But the Greatest of These Is Love

But the Greatest of These Is Love

Debbie Barrow Michael

Inspiring Voices®
A Service of **Guideposts**

Inspiring Voices books may be ordered through booksellers or by contacting:

Inspiring Voices
1663 Liberty Drive
Bloomington, IN 47403
www.inspiringvoices.com
1-(866) 697-5313

ISBN: 978-1-4624-0253-3 (e)
ISBN: 978-1-4624-0254-0 (sc)

Library of Congress Control Number: 2012914438

Printed in the United States of America

Inspiring Voices rev. date: 8/27/2012

To my mother, Nell Caskey—my first and best friend.

To Bruce, Heather, Kellie, Taylor, and Roma. I couldn't have chosen a better family; for that reason, I am thankful God did the choosing.

To the students of Linganore High School, past and present. What an unexpected blessing it has been to hang out with teenagers.

I love you all.

Introduction

When I started writing this manuscript ten years ago, I didn't know it would grow into a *real* book. I began recording the events of this story to preserve them from the black hole of my middle-aged memory. Before I knew how it happened, I was typing like one obsessed, sometimes being yanked out of bed at night with new insights, new perspectives of the story I was living. Seemingly unrelated ideas merged together in a stream of enlightened connectedness. At times it seemed as if I were simply typing dictation, as if I were the ghostwriter conveying the story God was telling me—no pressure there!

Years ago, Mother Teresa said, "I am a little pencil in the hand of a writing God who is sending a love letter to the world." Maybe God wants each of us to hold our little pencils and write love letters. This book is not really *my* story, nor is it *Roma's* story. It is one example of God's many love letters. I hope I have done this one justice.

Most people have read or heard the "Love" passage found in the thirteenth chapter of First Corinthians. It is often read at weddings, as it was at my own, but the lovely verses cannot truly change our lives until they are put into practice. The love-in-action part is hard.

> "If I speak in the tongues of men or of angels, but
> do not have love, I am only a resounding gong or a

clanging cymbal. If I have the gift of prophecy and can fathom all mysteries and all knowledge, and if I have a faith that can move mountains, but do not have love, I am nothing. If I give all I possess to the poor and give over my body to hardship that I may boast, but do not have love, I gain nothing.

Love is patient, love is kind. It does not envy, it does not boast, it is not proud. It does not dishonor others, it is not self-seeking, it is not easily angered, it keeps no record of wrongs. Love does not delight in evil but rejoices with the truth. It always protects, always trusts, always hopes, always perseveres.

Love never fails. But where there are prophecies, they will cease; where there are tongues, they will be stilled; where there is knowledge, it will pass away. For we know in part and we prophesy in part, but when completeness comes, what is in part disappears. When I was a child, I talked like a child, I thought like a child, I reasoned like a child. When I became a man, I put the ways of childhood behind me. For now we see only a reflection as in a mirror; then we shall see face to face. Now I know in part; then I shall know fully, even as I am fully known. And now these three remain: faith, hope and love. But the greatest of these is love." (NIV)

Someone once suggested that we start at the "Love is patient" part and substitute our names for "love." I tried it: "Debbie is patient, Debbie is kind, Debbie does not envy, nor boast, nor is proud." I couldn't say any of it with a straight face—not about *this* Debbie!

I can more easily identify with the beginning of the passage: I have often been a clanging cymbal. I can speak out for the disadvantaged people of the world—as long as they remain on the other side of the world, or at least outside my personal realm. I can give to the poor—as long as the poor do not move into my house.

Love is altogether different. Love has the potential to break my heart. Love leaves me vulnerable and exposed. Love is total surrender. God wants total surrender. God wants my eyes on Him following Him into places I cannot go by myself. Only when we totally surrender can He produce in us something so beyond what is humanly possible.

I can relate to Saint Peter who, like me, had experiences of unfathomable faith followed by paralyzing panic. "Get out of the boat and follow me," Jesus coaxed while walking on water. Peter stepped out onto the water and walked! But he immediately took his eyes off Jesus and sank, flailing faithlessly. *He* was an eye witness to Jesus' miraculous works, but how quickly he forgot what Jesus could do. Surely Peter should have been able to trust Jesus' power. Surely Peter more so than *I*.

I have also walked in the footsteps of doubting Thomas. In fact, the Bible is full of people with checkered spiritual pasts like my own. Jonah whined because he didn't want to help God save the Ninevites; Moses whined because he wanted God to send someone else to rescue the Israelites from slavery in Egypt. And I whine because obedience is sometimes too hard. If God was able to use these reluctant members of the Saints Hall of Fame who vacillated in their faith, then maybe he can use me too.

God has taught me lessons about love during this adventure. Love is indeed costly. Yet, love brings unparalleled joy, and love is the *only* thing that can heal a broken heart and mend a shattered life.

As you read, I hope you will imagine yourself walking in my shoes. My journey into faith, hope, and love certainly has had its peaks and valleys, but according to the Bible, I am in excellent company.

"*Never be frightened at your own faint-heartedness in attaining love . . . for love in action is a harsh and dreadful thing compared with love in dreams. Love in dreams is greedy for immediate action, rapidly performed and in the sight of all. But active love is labor and fortitude . . . just when you see with horror that in spite of all your efforts you are getting farther from your goal instead of nearer to it—at that very moment I predict that you will reach it and behold clearly the miraculous power of the Lord who has been all the time loving and mysteriously guiding you.*"

Fyodor Dostoevsky,
The Brothers Karamazov

Chapter One

"The heavens declare the glory of God; the
skies proclaim the work of his hands."

Psalm 19:1 (NIV)

April 22, 2002: I sat in a speechless daze on an idling plane on a remote runway at Washington Dulles International Airport. The enormous jets were lined up single file waiting their turn to depart. Out my window, a small American flag waved briskly from a pile of rusty, abandoned airport machinery. Just seven months earlier, terrorists had transformed a typical September morning into 9/11, a date that will forever symbolize ultimate hate. The flag was a sudden reminder of all that is noble in America. Since then, I, like many Americans, have been a little more passionate about our homeland and our flag. Overcome by an unexpected wave of love, patriotism, and fear, my eyes filled with tears. The lump was there in my throat, the proverbial physical clutch that embodied my emotional and spiritual panic. But my emotions were on overload for reasons beyond nostalgia; my entire life was about to change in a dramatic and permanent way.

I glanced at my watch again, 6:32 p.m., two minutes behind our scheduled departure. My impatience reflected my anxieties, and there were many. Might there still be time to run from the plane?

1

But the hulking Aeroflot jet lurched forward voiding the impulse. I looked out my window, wondering if I would ever see this land again or if life would ever return to normal. With the roar of those massive engines firing, the speed increased, and the forward thrust seemed to glue me to my seat. There was a terrifying and exhilarating realization that my fate was in someone else's hands. Then with a gentle lift, we were off.

No turning back now.

As the ground fell away beneath us, I began to have second thoughts about what had led me to this point. I had stubbornly given my husband no choice but to leave our three children at home with neighbors so we could travel half way around the world for what suddenly seemed like a crazy idea. What had I been thinking?

Was it just this morning that I had kissed my half-grown children goodbye before they left for school? Mechanically, I had rushed around all morning tending to final errands, remembering insurance information and noting instructions for sports and school activities. I drove to our small bank branch, regretting waiting until the last minute in case they didn't have the five thousand dollars in new, crisp one-hundred-dollar bills we were required to carry. The teller counted out the very last of the C-notes from her drawer. Another cryptic confirmation from God?

I delivered the latest copy of our will to my close friend and neighbor, not daring to think of the implications of that errand. Somewhere along the way, someone had advised us to fly on separate planes, as insurance against the unthinkable, a precaution for the biological children left at home during our journey to rescue the one God would not let me forget. In the chaos of the preparations, and with the unsettling fear of flying alone for twelve hours, my harried mind had rejected the suggestion. My husband, Bruce, and I would make this journey side by side, for better or for worse.

With the cash in my purse, more cash than I had carried in all my forty-six years, I had come skidding back into the house at one o'clock, just as my in-laws arrived take us to the airport. Our home in suburban Maryland was an hour from the airport, longer if there were traffic complications. We were instructed to arrive at the airport three hours before our scheduled departure to accommodate the new, heightened security procedures. I was more than willing to be scrutinized along with the other passengers. After mad men had steered plane-missiles into the Pentagon, and the Twin Towers of the World Trade Center, and wrestled with American heroes on a fourth lost plane, I welcomed the precautions.

For the past few months, I had been in a hypnotic daze, simply putting one foot in front of the other. Even so, those months had been peaceful and hopeful compared to the anxious turbulence of the prior year and a half, when I had bucked and resisted every hint from God about this assignment. My fear had often sent me into familiar, recurring tailspins of self-doubt, self-pity, and sometimes deep despair. Bruce had been stable during these last months, reassuring and supportive, even though he, by accepting this mission, had potentially more to lose than I did.

My husband had been well aware of my brittle emotional state before this recent calm settled over me. Since January I had successfully ignored the terror that loomed just below the surface in my subconscious. Bruce was not aware that a hidden spark of fear continued to smolder; nor did he realize how close to the surface that danger lurked. Suddenly, my uncertainties began to flare again, as I was reminded that our lives were in jeopardy, as well as the peace of our family, our marriage, my life as I knew it. And it had been a wonderful life—too wonderful to disrupt.

That indescribable sadness and fear which I had come to expect gripped me again. I looked out the window at the gray scenery and turned my face away from Bruce. He would not guess I was wavering yet again, too late this time. I took several deep breaths and wiped away the tears that blurred the scenery.

It was an overcast evening in our nation's capital. Watching the landscape shrink abruptly below us, I felt like a giant looking down on a world I did not recognize, that I did not belong to. I thought of my mother. Twenty-five years had whizzed by, separating me from the carefree existence of my youth in North Carolina. Life had once been simple. How did I get to this place?

Far below, thousands of toy cars lined up on ribbon roads during rush hour, squirming home to families. Where was my family? Were they, too, suddenly feeling this sobering sense of the inevitable reality and permanence of our mission? The heaviness in my throat and chest made me wish that I could collapse into the self-absorbed wailing of a sobbing session. More deep breaths. If we were on the right path, why did I feel so lost? Had I imagined this calling, this persistent urging that would not be ignored?

We rose into the thick clouds and everything below suddenly vanished. We were enclosed in suffocating whiteness. The turbulence reminded me of the physical danger we were in, as well as my emotional anguish. Then we broke through the clouds and entered the bright sunshine and blue sky of a spring evening in the heavens. The clouds below us were a dense carpet of enormous white fluff in all directions. Now, instead of feeling like a giant, I felt small and insignificant.

As I looked out my window to the east, there on a distant cumulus cloud was a perfect shadow of our plane. Framing it was a complete circular rainbow. I held my breath as I studied the fragile mirage. I would have grabbed my camera, but I could not look away, fearing the scene would vanish.

"Look Bruce—!" I said without taking my eyes from the window. My voice was hopeful, canceling my momentary panic.

"Yes, Deb?" he answered, gently squeezing my hand.

I pointed out my window. "Look. It's like a shield around the plane." I held my breath, hoping he saw it too, that it wasn't my imagination.

"Uh huh." He was unimpressed as he leaned toward my window and squinted to see. "It's probably something in the glass," he said, thinking I needed an explanation.

My dear husband of twenty-four years is a scientist, and this spectacle, like everything else he had ever seen in his life, had a logical explanation. I had hidden from him how close to a meltdown I'd been since we'd boarded the plane. He couldn't guess how desperately I needed a sign.

But he had *seen* it. And that was important to me. I had a witness when I would tell about that rainbow when we returned, and I *would* tell about it. To me the scene was nothing short of a miracle, like so many I had experienced since this whole journey had begun two years earlier. I felt God whispering, "Everything will be okay." I grabbed on to that promise.

God had not always whispered to me. There had been many moments, in fact, hours, days, and sleepless nights of doubt and seeming silence from God. When He *did* speak, I had turned my face away, afraid to listen, terrified to obey. But always, often when I least expected, He would shine an ever brighter light in the direction He had mapped out for me. I simply needed to stay alert, and be brave enough to take the small steps, one at a time, to follow the path God had prepared.

My mood changed to elation, though, from recent experience, I feared it would, too soon, change again. But for the moment, I smiled and settled back to enjoy the flight. My cup running over with unreasonable joy, I was mesmerized by the vision. The shadow and its rainbow gradually disappeared as we traveled in the opposite direction of the sun, and into the night.

During the next nine days of our journey, when my darkest doubts crept back to the surface, and the anxiety of uncertainty threatened once again to consume me, I would remember the view from my plane window. I would hold on to that nod from God reminding me that we were in His circle of care. The memory comforted me and upheld me. Like the tattered flag waving goodbye on the runway, the rainbow round our plane would be a familiar symbol to cling to in a foreign and foreboding land.

Chapter Two

"Do not be afraid—I will save you.
I have called you by name—
you are mine.
When you pass through deep
waters, I will be with you;
your troubles will not overwhelm you."

Isaiah 43:1–2 (GNT)

better start at the beginning, though I am not sure I can identify the exact moment of truth, or insight, or panic that signaled this turning point in my life. I could not recognize at the beginning of this journey that I had stepped out on a few safe stones in a gentle stream. Those stones would eventually become slippery and wobbly, sometimes submerging altogether to leave me stranded and crying out for help. A vague path seemed to be emerging before me, but to what destination and why? When the loose stones first shifted uncomfortably beneath my wary feet, I became alert, but I was helpless to return to the complacency of the shore. I could hear the roar of the waterfalls ahead and see the rapids covering the stones at times. The fear of being pulled down stream was terrifying. I could not walk on water, but I knew of Someone who could.

My 2002 journey to the airport and ultimately half way around the world started in 1999. A series of seemingly unconnected events, those stepping stones, set me in a direction that appeared innocuous, even alluring, until I was so far down the path I could not retreat. Ironically, in retrospect, one tragic incident stands out as a catalyst for the many changes that were to come.

In May of 1999, a favorite high school teacher of both my daughters lost her husband unexpectedly. Mrs. Inge was one of my favorite people. My association with her at that point had been limited to my attending school conferences and chaperoning art field trips. She was one of those rare types who exude warmth and friendliness, drawing new acquaintances immediately into her circle of friendship as if she had loved them all her life. And she adored my girls. How could I not love her?

Heather, a senior, and Kellie, a freshman, were heartbroken for their beloved mentor. Although they didn't know Ed Inge, they were desperate to soothe his wounded wife. We called her, visited her, sent flowers and a card. Even I was compelled to do more. I had an idea: I would offer to help with her classes while she took some much needed personal leave. She taught drawing and painting classes, and I had a drawing and painting degree. Instead of a random substitute teacher covering her classes, I could help for the few remaining weeks of the school year so she wouldn't have to worry about her students' unfinished masterpieces. The grieving teacher was touched and pleased with my idea.

I called the school to see if I could volunteer to be her substitute. The secretary in the office told me the only way I could teach her classes was to register with the county school system as a substitute teacher. I didn't want to be a sub. I just wanted to help in a voluntary capacity; nevertheless, the high school directed me to the Frederick County Public Schools substitute coordinator who informed me it was too late in the school year to become a substitute. The department would offer no more orientations for subs until the fall. I was instructed to contact them in August. I would not be allowed to help Anne Inge; her classes had already been assigned a substitute for the remainder of the school year.

When school started in the fall of 1999, Kellie, then a tenth grader, continued to pursue the subbing idea. Anne Inge, back in her classroom, didn't need me anymore, but substitute teachers were in short supply, especially at the high school level.

"I really think you would love it, Mom," Kellie would coax.

I did not want to be a sub, but the option did have some benefits. Heather had just left for her freshman year at Maryland Institute, College of Art, in Baltimore. Kellie had three years left of high school. My son, Taylor, was in the fifth grade. I had not worked at a full-time job since the kids were born. I was reluctant to start again, but substitute teaching was part-time. I wouldn't have to accept assignments every day. I could still be home when my children were home.

I have to admit I have always enjoyed teenagers in small groups. At neighborhood, school, and church events, I usually migrate away from the adults toward the teenagers to hear about the challenges and dramas that fill their lives with both angst and excitement. Their energy and optimism are magnetic; their needs unleashed the most empathetic listener in me. As I thought about my fondness for adolescents, I decided I might try it. I would apply . . . later. I spent the fall immersed in my own art—preparing my one-of-a-kind, hand-sculpted Santas, elves, and angels for the Maryland Christmas Show.

My sculpting ability had not been encouraged or appreciated when I was younger. As a senior in college, I had taken sculpting as an elective in summer school. To my utter surprise and dismay, I failed the class. Failure didn't come easily to me. I didn't believe I deserved an F. We sculpted from live models, and I thought mine looked as much like the model as anyone else's, and more so than most. But apparently realism was not the goal in a class where abstract expressionism was revered. I had given up my sculpting tools and any desire to create three-dimensional art. For almost twenty years, I didn't touch a piece of clay. In 1995, I had picked up a carton of the new polymer clay and a doll magazine. After my family had retired for the evening (so there would be no witnesses if I failed again), I sculpted a face. I was thrilled when the tiny, detailed face seemed to grow out of the clay almost without my efforts. I left the shrunken head on the kitchen table for my family to discover at breakfast. I delighted in their wide-eyed astonishment.

The next week I cautiously sculpted three more, every time fearing it was an accident, and I would not be able to create another. My sculpting teacher was wrong; I did have some talent! I lovingly built bodies for them out of wire and quilt batting, dressed them and put them into environments on boards with toys, antiques, or other props. At a local doll shop, the finished vignettes attracted quite of bit of attention. I was encouraged, though they were so labor-intensive, I knew I would never make much money from their sales. But some was better than none, and I was vindicated, as far as a twenty-year-old memory of failure in sculpture class was concerned.

After the holidays, Kellie resumed her mission, eliciting Bruce's help this time, in her quest to convince me to substitute teach. Even Taylor suggested that I could sub in his class at the elementary school. Now everyone in my family thought this was a great idea. With one child in college and another preparing to go, Bruce was ready for me to be employed, and he could be extremely persuasive. Having not worked for so many years, I felt that Bruce might have to pry my fingers from the door jambs to make me leave my snug and comfortable home. I did not like the pressure I felt my family putting on me. And I suddenly felt "uncalled" to teach at a public high school. I could teach art, maybe, but what about algebra, or physics, or Spanish? I had taken five years of French in high school, but French spoken with a southern accent might be an altogether different foreign language to these Yankees in Maryland!

Originally, I had just wanted to help Anne Inge. Until her

husband died, the idea of being a substitute teacher had never crossed my mind. The prospect was so outside my comfort zone, I no longer wanted to consider it. My family's persistence sent me into retreat mode. I burrowed in at home, determined not to venture into the high school realm. I might enjoy young people, one on one, but I did not like being the center of attention nor speaking in front of groups. I always declined invitations to talk at school meetings, or art clubs, or even to read scripture at church on Sunday morning. "That is not my gift," I had grown comfortable repeating and justified in declining. I had convinced myself that my aversion to public speaking was less of a fear and more of a personality trait. I would leave the lime light for those who thrived there. I much preferred the shadows of backstage.

Reality presented another stepping stone in my path. The dwindling of Heather's college savings after only one semester became an incentive I could not ignore. I had earned a small fraction of her tuition with my hand-sculpted dolls. People loved them at the show; my booth was like a museum—people came through and marveled, but few purchased. And my new craft was seasonal. I needed something regular.

Kellie's gently persistent pep talks encouraged me that I might possess adequate skills to monitor a high school class. Her love inspired me because she wanted me to be at *her* school, among *her* friends. Infused with Kellie's confidence in me, I attended the orientation for substitutes at the end of January 2000—with no obligation, I reminded myself. I was fingerprinted, completed the requisite paperwork, and ordered my transcripts. My procrastination was aided by bureaucratic bumbling: my transcripts got lost. The college sent them under my maiden name, so the board of education filed them away in the vast bureaucratic vacuum where lost papers reside. After a few weeks, the problem was solved; finally, I was registered in the Frederick County Substitute Information Management System. I waited for the phone to ring. Weeks went by, but no one seemed to need me after all.

About the time I was surrendering to the subbing suggestion, I heard that small-group Bible studies were starting at my church. The text, *Experiencing God*, by Henry Blackaby, had come highly recommended by two women in my Sunday school class. I expressed a slight interest. I was cautious because I never participated in Bible studies. I rarely read anymore, except an occasional magazine article, or headlines in the daily newspaper. I didn't meet in groups that might cause me discomfort. I attended church and adult Sunday school on Sundays, every Sunday, with my family, and that was enough. I was on a few committees at church that took about as much time as I could spare. I prayed, sometimes. As survey polls suggest, like the majority of Americans, I considered myself a Christian.

Experiencing God arrangements were made, and suddenly I didn't have time to back out. I was swept up in a Bible study. Carol and Sarah, the advocates of the book, had raved about it. It was "life changing" they had said with wide eyes. I didn't tell them, but I didn't *want* my life to change. It was perfect.

I halfheartedly read my first week's lesson, but I was immediately intrigued by what I read in the book's preface. The text almost leaped from the page. It said, "We do not find God's will; it is revealed. God always takes the initiative." Besides sounding like less work for me, this philosophy sounded fascinating, even magical. But at our first meeting, our leader directed our attention to a paragraph that read: "If I do everything He says, I will be in the center of His will when He wants to use me for a special assignment." I turned to Teri, a woman for whom I had considerable respect, and whispered, unashamed, "I don't want an assignment!"

"I don't either," she answered matter-of-factly.

Big assignments were for other people, for those who felt "called." I had never felt "called," didn't want to be called. My life was just fine. More than fine; it was wonderful.

Two weeks into our Wednesday morning study, Bruce suggested I attend one of the evening study groups instead, so that when I started to get calls to sub, I would be available. Daytime meetings had been a habit for me, so I could be home in the evenings with my family. Bruce's suggestion had merit, and having an evening out sounded exciting. The kids were older with interests and activities of their own. Seeing me involved with my own interests would be beneficial to them, especially a church activity. I wanted them to have some "religion" in their lives.

I learned two women were starting a nighttime study of *Experiencing God*. One was a close friend, and I looked forward to doing anything with her. Her name was also Debbie, and we had worked on several decorating jobs and stage sets around the church and community. The other woman, Gretta, was a newcomer to my Sunday school class. Both of these ladies exuded "fun." I wanted in on that! I saw them at church on Sunday morning and asked if I might join them.

The new millennium had brought changes to my world—I was no longer a stay-at-home mom where my entire existence had revolved around raising three children and being available for my family. I was about to launch a new job and an evening out, even if it was disguised as a Bible study. Neither the job nor the lesson reading appeared to be too taxing; I still maintained a measure of control.

Chapter Three

"Above all the grace and the gifts that Christ
gives his beloved is that of overcoming self."

Saint Francis of Assisi

Originally I saw this Bible study as, first, a social event and second, a self-improvement opportunity. However, almost from the beginning, *Experiencing God* held a mysterious attraction for me. The reading was intense. It seemed as though God was speaking directly to me. Blackaby's words coaxed me out onto the dry, firm rocks of my new path. It was comfortable there, and I congratulated myself on venturing out. I did not detect the raging water yet; any encounter with risk was a safe distance away. Even though the reading selections sometime made me uneasy, I mechanically took another step onto the next stone. I could not retreat. That far-off rumbling of a dramatic change drew me forward. *Experiencing God* spoke to my spirit; the rest of me was not listening yet!

Our study group planned to meet for an hour each week and discuss our estimated twenty-minutes-per-day readings. The author, in no uncertain terms, suggested that if I wasn't hearing God speak to me, there was something wrong with my relationship with God. Of course there was a problem—I didn't have that personal love relationship with God that the book described. I had never even expected it, until now. I cried out to God when I needed some help, but I put Him back on the shelf, out of the way, when life was going smoothly. He wasn't a part of my everyday life. I tried to be a decent person, and I was comfortably religious, but lately I was aware that there was something lacking.

The nighttime schedule worked out great for many reasons, one being that I was getting calls to sub every day.

My first day of substituting at the end of February 2000, was not at the high school, as I had expected, but at New Market Middle School. I arrived at the office early, got my assignment, and sat at the teacher's desk in the empty room. Shortly before the bell rang to begin the day, I was stricken with panic. I remembered again why I did not want to be a substitute teacher. I did not like to speak in front of groups. I was shy and self-conscious when all eyes were on me. I did not like to try new ventures where there was the possibility of failure.

I looked out at the silent rows of desks, realizing that soon most, if not all, of those seats would be occupied by seventh graders, maybe even disrespectful, mean-spirited kids who would smell my fear and attack like pit bulldogs unleashed in a meat market.

One friend had questioned my sanity when I told her that I was going to sub.

"You are too nice. They will eat you alive," she predicted, unsympathetically.

I did not want to be breakfast for these little cannibals! I took deep breaths and consoled myself with the fact that, good or bad, the day would end, and I would never have to return again. I could do anything for one day. I knew Bruce and Kellie would be disappointed in me for giving up too soon.

The bell rang. The students clattered in, and I heard my own voice emerging from the morning routine of book bags being unzipped, notebooks flopping open, chitchat between friends, sniping between adversaries, and desks shuffling into position.

"Good morning class." I heard my most cheerful voice say as they quieted down. "Mr. Brown will not be here today. I am Mrs. Michael."

Somehow they didn't notice the thunderous beating of my heart or the taut strain in my voice from nerves strung too tight. These were pleasant and courteous kids. They respected me as an authority figure, even if I didn't see myself in that capacity. There was the roll to call and worksheets to distribute, instructions to give, even occasional suggestions to offer. The kids were courteous enough, especially one tiny boy named Anthony. He volunteered to help with anything I needed. He told me names of absent students and helped me distribute papers. The students were all eager to be helpful when I told them this was my first day. They seemed pleased when I told them at the end of each class that they had made my first day of subbing enjoyable. I shared that I would leave their teacher a good report about their behavior. By lunchtime I felt comfortable, almost smug about how well my day had gone so far. I might survive to return another day. Maybe subbing wasn't too horrible; to the contrary, I was infused with enthusiasm and self confidence.

Little Anthony returned for a small, special education class in Mr. Brown's room in the afternoon, and jumped right back into the role of being my "assistant." He enjoyed the opportunity to be a helper, and I so appreciated his help and kindness that I promised myself to acknowledge his thoughtfulness with a note of thanks.

In the days that followed, I had many calls to replace teachers at the high school. My first morning at Linganore High School was disheartening. I arrived a half hour before school started. I was cautiously optimistic, but the activity in the hallways awakened me to the realities of high school life. My vanity had assured me that they would like me if they got to know me, but that was a whopping "if."

Students lumbered down the hallways, still half asleep. They ignored my attempts to be friendly, the same efforts that had rewarded me with the middle-school students' trust. Not yet knowing where the staff restroom was, I crossed the threshold of forbidden territory—the girls' smoke-filled restroom. Never mind that cigarettes were contraband. One look at the suspicious faces told me that I was not welcomed. I backed out, nostrils burning, and informed a passing teacher of the smoking infraction.

Many of these kids had a hard edge to them, their spirits encrusted in hard shells. Most were bigger than I, and many had attitudes and vocabularies that were against the law at my house! I remembered the kinder, gentler kids in middle school, and I wondered if maybe that age group was a better fit for me. But Kellie wanted me at the high school, at *her* school.

The kids entered my first period class, remedial Algebra I, still sleepy. They were apathetic toward me and unenthusiastic about the work their teacher left to complete. They put their heads down and were reluctant to attempt the equations. I couldn't physically make them do their work, and I didn't want to be confrontational on my first day. A group who sat close to the teacher's desk seemed willing to give me a chance. I unexpectedly found myself in the comfortable position of being in a small group setting, with the kids in the front of the class who were eager to show respect to a person they felt was in charge. I tried to help a few who were serious about passing algebra. I studied the book, pretending I had not forgotten the little algebra I had once known. Luckily I found enough examples in the text book to attempt to answer their questions. One girl, Jessica, with orange-blond hair and two-inch dark roots, volunteered to do problems on the board for examples, so the students could understand better. She answered their questions and proudly wrote strings of impressive looking equations.

"Wow, Jessica, you really know this stuff," I encouraged her.

"I failed it last semester. I don't want to take it again!" she said with the conviction of someone who had learned her lesson.

18

Jessica, Jessica, Jessica I repeated silently to myself, aware of my weakness for remembering names. I liked Jessica. She was a lovely girl once I talked to her. And Amanda, and John. I wanted to remember their names for the next time I had them in class.

In each of the classes I covered that day, I made a connection with a couple of students in this way, and when I left at the end of the day, I believed I had made some progress.

The second and third time I went to the high school, I was exposed to a different group of students: advanced classes. Some of the students were so intelligent, I felt that if I spoke at all, I would blow my cover and they would know instantly that they knew more than I did. Some of these young scholars were friends of my girls, so I talked comfortably to them and their friends. These were courteous, respectful, motivated young adults with bright futures. They carried out their assignments without my help. I was almost unnecessary.

On the fourth day when I walked into the classroom at Linganore High School, something remarkable happened. One of the students I had subbed for before asked hopefully, "Are you our sub?" When I answered affirmatively, he said, "Sweet!" Other students cheered too.

My vanity gorged itself! I was smug and self-satisfied. I naively thought they were glad to see *me*. I wouldn't understand until later that, in reality, they were simply delighted their teacher was absent. *Any* sub would have sufficed. To the students, my presence signaled a day to goof off and do nothing. But it gave me courage and self confidence to relax and enjoy their presence, because I thought they were enjoying mine! Sometimes ignorance *is* bliss!

The stones in my path led me through still waters. The changes in my life had not been so traumatic after all. I did not want to sub, but God knew what He was doing, even though I had not trusted Him and I had been self-centered and resistant at every turn. If this alteration in my life was the waterfall I had feared, I was finally eager for the challenge. I was firmly fastened in the raft, with life jacket buckled, ready to experience the thrill.

Chapter Four

"When Christ calls a man, he
bids him come and die."

Dietrich Bonhoeffer

After two weeks of subbing, I knew Kellie was right— I was going to love it. But I remembered I had not written that note to Anthony. With the high school kids to compare him to now, I truly appreciated his gentle kindness. His eagerness to please told me that he would like the attention. After a couple of days remembering and forgetting him, I finally sat down at the kitchen table one evening in early March to write a quick, encouraging, and sincere note. As I got to the end of my message, I wanted to say something like "your mom must be proud of you." Then I had a sudden thought—what if Anthony didn't have a mom. I froze, and my heart instantly ached for him at the idea. Okay, I would write "family" instead of "mom."

Then another abrupt thought, almost like a whisper, came from nowhere. It was more unsettling than thinking of Anthony being an orphan. Chills covered my arms and my neck hair prickled. It was not my thought. It might as well have been a neon sign, its impact on me was so vivid and the message was unmistakable. "Adoption." I sat paralyzed.

"What was that?" I asked the universe, as I sat attentive, expecting more clues.

"God, am I supposed to adopt Anthony?" I heard myself say aloud with my pen poised above the paper.

I did not *want* to adopt. Not Anthony, not anybody! At forty-four years of age, I already had all the children I ever hoped to have, and on some days, more than I wanted! "I'm sure Anthony has a mom—what a crazy impulse. I am taking this job way too seriously," I chided myself. I finished Anthony's note, using "family" instead of "mom." Certainly he had some kind of family, maybe even a foster family. I took it by the middle school the following day and left it with his teacher to deliver to him.

In the days that followed, I lost the overwhelming feeling that I was supposed to adopt Anthony. When I had reported to his teacher how helpful he had been, Mr. Brown had not related any sad orphan stories about the boy. I was relieved to assume that he was loved and cared for.

Although I had put Anthony's parentage to rest, I remained keenly aware of adoptions. That single, searing thought ushered in periods of anxiety that I had not previously known in my life. The word adoption haunted me. Over the next few months, dread lingered in the aftermath of the unexpected suggestion of adoption, and a debilitating fog of irresolution settled over my life.

I would turn on the television to an unexpected program about adoption. I would get in my car, turn on the radio, and hear something about European orphans. Other programs on the radio would feature parents of older adopted children. Time after time this happened. Maybe there had always been stories about adoption, but now I was *hearing* them. It sickened me. I did not *want* to adopt!

Sometimes I would sit down to relax and escape, and read my *Chicken Soup for the Mother's Soul* that Kellie had given me for my birthday. I would open it randomly to read, only to discover that the story I found was written by an adoptive mother. These experiences brought on overwhelming despair. I particularly was disturbed by the messages about older orphans, the ones who might be damaged from years of neglect and rejection. Maybe, if I had to, I could adopt a baby, an infant without all the scars from months and years of not being adored. But even that prospect did not excite me. I did not want to mother another child of any age!

That week my reading in *Experiencing God* was about becoming God-centered. A summary statement that was particularly distressing was: "I am a servant of God. I adjust my life to what He is about to do." If God's plan for me included adoption, I didn't want God to speak to me! I didn't want to be a servant if it meant bringing another child into my family.

My heart plummeted when I could plainly hear the rushing water downstream, threatening to trap me in dizzying whirlpools. Forget the life jacket. I would rather be sucked under and drown than to put my life in such excruciating turbulence. I would breathe in the water and welcome placid death.

"Please God, not *adoption*."

I could not raise another child. My family had been complete for years. Heather was eighteen, Kellie was almost sixteen, and Taylor was almost eleven. Not once had I considered adopting.

I had seen the news segments encouraging viewers to consider giving a local child a "forever home," usually children from the foster-care system with special needs and a lot of baggage, the ones whose heart-wrenching stories and pleading smiles would make a hardened criminal weep. I couldn't watch. Did God have one of these children in mind for me?

Another possibility, no less daunting, crept into my fearful mind. After the fall of communism in 1991, horrendous images of neglected children in state-run eastern European orphanages appeared in the media. The photos and publicity of the deplorable living conditions led to an international uproar and an outpouring of humanitarian aid. I was still haunted by the reports. Had God chosen one of those children to be mine?

How could I reach a child who had not trusted, who had no

reason to hope? I foresaw years of frustration stretching before me, endless sessions of therapy to fix a broken child and to restructure our formerly healthy family. I was afraid of the damage that such a child might bring to us. How could we teach a child to love if he didn't understand the concept, if he could not even comprehend the possibility? I imagined a rescued baby bird flapping in my hands, impotent and terrified, unfazed by any amount of stroking and soothing. There would be no words to make it understand that I was just trying to help. Weren't unloved, damaged children as fragile and frightened as the fallen sparrow? And weren't fallen sparrows God's problem? I did not want that kind of responsibility. I would fail. I was failing, just thinking about it.

Was I equipped to deal with a damaged fledgling? Was it fair to my family? Even if the answer to both questions was yes, I still did not *want* to do it. It was not that I simply was not interested; I was stubbornly opposed to mothering another child. My own children had few problems—I was their mother and they were, as a matter of fact, almost perfect, in my "unbiased" opinion! The multitude of problems that could exist in a child that was not my own precluded that I would never even consider such a risky undertaking. I had immense respect and admiration for the families that did take on these troubled kids, truly I did, but that was not my gift.

Chapter Five

"Each one of them is Jesus in disguise."

Mother Teresa

Hanging out with teenagers, on the other hand, felt like my calling, and it was a welcome distraction from unpleasant thoughts of motherless children. I was determined to throw myself into my new mission. Hadn't God clearly led me here? Although I was available to sub at both the middle and high schools, I particularly loved the older kids. In a school of 1400 students, I wondered how I would get to know them all, but I yearned to. As the first entry in my new prayer journal, I wrote, "Lord, help me remember their names." I needed divine intervention for this request—I seemed to have no memory bank for names. I wasn't even good at remembering faces.

Encouraging kids, learning their interests, joking with them—this is what I enjoyed when they were visiting my children at our home. I was always glad to see these same kids at school. And I was meeting many more who I wanted my quiet Kellie, who still had two and a half years left of high school, to know better. But now I was exposed to a whole new group of kids, kids who my own girls would have been afraid to bring home as new friends, fearing their mother's reaction! Names I had only heard spoken in fear or distaste over the years were suddenly *my* friends! My daughters thought it was funny that the kids they considered delinquents were talking to me in the halls and during class. That somehow made me "cool." I genuinely liked those square pegs, the unique students who were on the radar screen in the principal's office. I was determined they would feel my affection. I remembered them from class to class. I remembered they had taken an important test the last day I subbed for them, or that they had a pivotal game that afternoon. I remembered the details of their lives. And amazingly, I remembered their names. This skill seemed to fascinate them, and please them. Everyone wants to be memorable. I would call them by name as we passed in the hall, and suddenly there was a bond between us. When someone calls you by name, you know you are recognized, acknowledged, and important.

Sometimes a wayward student would pass my classroom door, give an excited wave, duck in, and pull up a chair beside me to talk. This was unacceptable behavior in the middle of class when they were supposed to be elsewhere. I would make sure they were okay, and then hurry them on to their intended destination, before they, or I, got into trouble. Almost predictably, when I walked into a particularly difficult class, one of the usual ringleaders would make an announcement to the class, "Hey Mizz Michael. Mizz Michael loves me, don't you?" Some of the quieter students would look at me in disbelief.

"Somebody has to!" I would playfully affirm. Many times those new friends would get the class settled down by yelling over the noise, "Be nice for Mizz Michael," or more likely, "Will you guys shut up!" I was always thankful for their help, then I would let them be my "assistant" for the period.

I was sometimes realistic enough to know that my enviable rapport with the kids wasn't about *me*, or anything *I* did. It wasn't my bubbly personality. Anyone who listened to them and made an effort to know them, *anyone* who cared about them, would have been an instant success. I was grateful it was me. High school students were the perfect age for me because the students had adult senses of humor. They understood my quirky, sometimes sarcastic attempts at wit. They liked being the brunt of my jokes.

"Mizz Michael, I got my driver's license," proud students would boast almost daily, while passing me in the hall.

"That is scary. Thanks for the warning," I would answer without slowing down. Their delighted giggles echoed in the hall.

Often they would try to alter the lesson plans left by their teacher: "He told us to tell you to ignore that worksheet and just let us pick a movie to watch today."

"Not a chance. I am obviously smarter than I look." They might have been resourceful, but I was obviously . . . smarter than I looked!

"Well, can you say you lost the worksheet, or forgot about it? He'll never know. We'll back you up." They were persistent.

"Why does it have to be *my* negligence, or *my* carelessness? I'll just say you refused to do your work. I am a rule follower," I would announce slowly and deliberately. "I will give you the assignment as your teacher asked me to."

They didn't give up hope that I might one day relent and give them a break on their work, but someone would always speak up and say, "No, Mrs. Michael is a 'rule follower'" in the same slow, deliberate way I had said it, reminding their peers that begging would not weaken me.

"Please, please, please," they would beg when requesting something ridiculous, like ordering pizza or skipping out for McDonald's. Dramatically and persuasively, they would purse their hands as though in prayer.

"Does that work at your house?" I would ask incredulously.

"What?" they would ask, confused, as if they had forgotten what they were asking.

"Begging. It must work at your house; otherwise, you wouldn't try it. It doesn't work with me."

They enjoyed my friendly banter. It was a game. It implied a personal connection. They returned my teasing, respectfully, most of the time. They playfully imitated my southern accent, knowing that I was a proud North Carolinian. I was no longer intimidated standing and talking in front of them. I even noticed I was more comfortable talking in front of my peers after practicing on my young friends. In many ways, I gained more from our friendship than they did.

At first the classes in which I was most relaxed were not the advanced classes, though I was often relieved to have them because those students were self-motivated and required less maintenance. But the kids in those classes didn't *need* me to be there. I was unnecessary in those "think tanks," and I had little to contribute to the conversations of the brilliant. I felt more essential in classrooms where kids struggled at home, or with school, or with friends—kids who needed an advocate, or a mother. And there were too many kids like that.

Not every day was a great day. Some days I left school feeling beat-up, wondering how I could continue to show up. I was grouchy sometimes. Many students were disrespectful and ignorant of socially acceptable behavior. Sometimes I felt like running screaming from the building. They exhausted me. Many times I watched an unmoving clock stuck on a too-early hour. Usually, after a few days rest, my next visit to the school would remind me why I loved to be there.

Being a substitute teacher had many perks. One was there's usually time at the end of class just to talk. I am an observer of people, but sometimes I would be drawn into their conversations. I asked hard questions because I was interested; they confided in me because they wanted someone to care. These teenagers accepted me. They trusted me enough to share their secrets and their dreams and their fears. Usually all I had to do was listen and let my emotions be honest. They weren't looking to me to solve their problems; they just wanted someone who was willing to share their load.

I didn't have to be the disciplinarian, not at first anyway. That responsibility would have to be earned, when the students respected my fairness, and I trusted myself. But in my first few months as a substitute teacher, I could just be a resident "friend."

Chapter Six

"One act of obedience is better
than one hundred sermons."

Dietrich Bonhoeffer

Subbing at the middle school again one morning, I ran into a casual friend I had known for a decade or more. She worked at the school as an instructional aide. Our paths would cross periodically, and we always stopped to chat and catch up on news of our families. Our kids were close in ages.

She shared that she was down on her luck—her marriage was failing, and she had just bought an older used car to replace her ancient clunker that had simply worn out. She couldn't save any money and was sinking deeper and deeper into debt. She finished by telling me that she was actually counting lunch bags, hoping they would last until the end of the school year, because she couldn't afford to buy more. I stood there listening and aching. I couldn't imagine being in such a desperate personal and financial predicament.

As I was listening to her, I felt moved to give her money. Not then, but later, and she was not to know who gave it to her. She had just told me private information, but I knew I wasn't the only one who had heard her stories. She wasn't a whiner, but her life was an open book. I think it was therapy of sorts for her to share her hardships. As we parted, I wished her luck and hugged her. I was immediately sorry I hadn't told her that I would pray for her, but that impulse was a new one since my study of *Experiencing God* had begun. Before, I would have feared putting someone off with the offer. But it is just as well that I kept quiet; otherwise, it might have tipped her off to my inspired plan.

All during the morning, I strongly felt God telling me to give her one hundred dollars. One hundred dollars! I only made seventy dollars a day, before taxes, and was eager to be paid that meager sum. But I did feel clear and strangely excited about the mission.

About lunchtime, I started to have doubts. *One hundred dollars? How would she spend it?* Probably not as carefully as I would! I was the coupon queen, and Bruce was tighter than two coats of paint. I would give her *fifty* dollars, and she would be thrilled to get it!

And another thing, I wanted her to know who gave it to her.

At that point, I realized Satan was trying to steal my joy. There was a battle going on inside me over right and wrong, good and bad, obedience and disobedience. I finally resolved to be obedient. But during the day and evening, the battle was waged again, and again. Before I lost the war, I went by the bank to cash my check. I put five crisp twenty-dollar bills into an envelope with a card in which I wrote, "I hope this is the answer to prayer, so consider it a gift from God."

Although I didn't work the next day, I drove to the school and put my card in her mailbox in the office. I felt utter joy as I imagined her finding it and wondering who her benefactor was. Every person with whom she came in contact could be a possible candidate. It must have changed the way she looked at people. I knew it was the right thing to do, and how she spent it was her concern.

That evening I received another "message" from God as I was opening the mail. One note was from a friend who had wanted to repay me for repairing one of my sculptures she had purchased, the finger of a Santa her grandson had broken off. I had fixed it as a favor, six months earlier. I didn't want any money to make the fifteen minute repair. But here, half a year later, was a gift certificate to a favorite local restaurant for $25. In the same batch of mail was a check for $25, a rebate on a computer game I had sent in so long ago, I had lost any hope of ever receiving it. And finally, I opened an envelope addressed to Bruce (forgive me) from the State of Maryland, with a reimbursement check in the amount of $52. Bruce was a State employee. Three checks worth $102 lay before me. I understood the significance immediately. Bruce bent over my shoulder to look at his check.

"Huh," he said. "I don't even remember putting in a claim for that."

How could Bruce understand? He didn't have all the information, all the pieces of the puzzle. He didn't even know there *was* a puzzle. I would tell him about the money sometime. I was afraid to examine or divulge these stirrings from God too soon. To me, the three checks verified that the hundred dollars I had begrudgingly given to a desperate friend had really been from God after all—He had reimbursed me.

I recognized this incident as an "opportunity" to be the servant Christian. The experience of God's blessings and compensation for my reluctant and feeble attempts at obedience put me on the path, at least for short bursts of time, of trusting and obeying. Little missions for God were not so costly, and the rewards were great. I felt unreasonable joy over such simple matters. I *could* be an ambassador for God. If God wanted me for these mini-assignments, I was willing, even enthusiastic.

The water was a cheerful, babbling brook, with no threatening sound from dangerous rapids ahead . . . maybe because I had my fingers in my ears!

Chapter Seven

"Trust in the Lord with all your heart; do not depend on your own understanding. Seek his will in all you do, and he will direct your paths."

Proverbs 3:5–6 (NIV)

Our family had become acquainted with Jacki and Steve Tate a few years earlier through our daughters' friendship. They were Christians, committed, practicing Christians. We rarely saw them, so their call in April came as a surprise. They invited Bruce and me to a banquet for a group called Youth for Christ (YFC), sometimes known as Campus Life, a name the kids found less intimidating. The Tates sponsored this group financially. YFC's message was designed to reach "unchurched" youth. Subbing at the high school, I knew the kids they were trying to reach. Meg, a wonderful woman from our church, was also at the banquet, helping the kids from our high school district with their presentations for the evening.

As I listened to the speakers share what Campus Life meant to me, it occurred to me that maybe this was where God was leading me. After all, wasn't it odd that the Tate's invited us here? I really didn't have any extra time, what with my new job and Bible study, but this would be a lot easier than permanently bringing a child into my home and worse, my heart. The thought of adoption continued to linger, but I mentioned it to no one, fearing that talking about it would somehow move me closer to acting on the idea. I was considering that maybe God wanted me to do something *like* adoption. Getting involved in the lives of children was probably what He had in mind.

A couple of days after the banquet, I called Meg to see if she needed help on Monday nights. As I suspected, she did.

Gary was the leader of the group. Meg and I helped wherever we were needed. Sometimes we would help lead small groups; other times we were just damage- and crowd-controllers. Any job was fine with me. I now had another mini-assignment that I could live with.

The name "Youth for Christ" might imply they were a group of nice young people seeking to learn more about God. In reality, many of the kids who attended on Monday nights were the same troubled kids I knew from school. They were involved with alcohol, drugs, and casual sex, some had even been to jail. It was interesting to me that they knew where to come for love and support and to get answers to some of life's hard questions. I invited and picked up a few of the students I thought would benefit from the fellowship and small group discussions. The conversations were lively at times. My love for them and my maternal manner were offset by my honest astonishment and bewilderment. I loved *them* but not their behavior. I was aware my eyes must be bulging at some of their stories and remarks.

Once, in a small group discussion, Erin tried to convince me that smoking weed was okay, that the Bible even condoned it, but she didn't know exactly where to find that passage.

I, of course, challenged her information.

She had argued this case before and had practiced her testimony.

"Weed is God-made. Nothing is added to it. I wouldn't smoke anything made by man, I *do* have scruples," she smugly asserted.

"Erin, God made poison ivy too, but you wouldn't want to smoke it!" I countered.

I was aware that I didn't convince Erin. She didn't want to be convinced. Her self-centered desires were all the evidence she needed. But perhaps seeds were planted somewhere.

And Katharine's boyfriend didn't want to use condoms because it was against his religion. It was apparently *not* against his religion to have premarital sex! I was always amazed by their convictions of convenience!

And cheating on tests was okay, because it didn't hurt anyone.

"What if you go to college and have to sign an honor code stating you 'have neither given nor received help on this exam.' Will you sign it?" I thought I was asking a thought-provoking question.

"Of course," one girl answered immediately, as if my question was ludicrous, "I wouldn't incriminate myself by *not* signing it." Almost everyone agreed with her.

(I hoped my doctor hadn't gotten through medical school with that philosophy!)

These were the debates I had to be prepared for, not just on Monday nights, but every day at school. I was there, not merely to be their friend, but also to be a witness to their behavior so they would hold themselves accountable. Often they would censor themselves: "Sorry Mizz Michael," they would say to me after bad language seemed to involuntarily spew from their lips. I would flop my head down like a rag doll in an exaggerated expression of disappointment and exasperation.

"What would your mother say if she heard you say that?" I have often scolded my young friends in my slow, thicker-than-usual southern accent which I summon as needed for emphasis.

And often their answer has been the same.

"This is the way my mother talks."

The school became my mission field. I think God wanted me there. This was probably what He meant—*love* them almost *as if* they were my own. I was okay with that, as long as I didn't have to take them home with me!

On days when subs were monitoring class, the workload was often lighter, resulting in extra time for general discussions to break out around the classroom. Sometimes these discussions would digress into religious debates. I would draw nearer, aware that in this secular society, I had to be careful about my comments, and not appear to proselytize. Now that I loved my job, I wanted to keep it.

"I know we are not supposed to talk about religion at school," one student finally said, searching my face for . . . approval? . . . permission?

"Don't *ever* feel that you have to leave your faith at the front door when you enter school," I responded. "It is absolutely legal for you to have religious discussions at school. I just can't initiate them, or add to the discussion. In the law's eyes, it would be wrong for me to preach to you. But I can certainly listen to your interesting discussion, and nod in agreement occasionally," I added, smiling.

During one of these debates one day, I kind of broke the rule, even though I am a rule follower. Betsy, who was Kellie's friend, was talking about God. Andrew, a proud, self-proclaimed atheist was ridiculing her belief in the tooth fairy, Santa Claus, and God. They went back and forth for a while. Betsy knew my faith well, and invited me to share a thought on the subject.

I spoke deliberately and slowly, "I have absolutely no doubt whatsoever that God exists."

Andrew swung around and faced me with, not hostility, but *pleading* in his eyes. "How?"

This young man was not so sure of his conviction after all. All eyes were suddenly on me as I smiled knowingly.

"Unfortunately I am forbidden to share my faith at school." I responded (a little after the fact!) By my indiscretion I had the opportunity to fertilize some seeds God planted that day.

A few days later one of the girls from the religion debate asked me to pray for her grandmother. I was touched that she trusted me to speak to God on her behalf. A secretary overheard her request. Later, the secretary opened up about her prayer life and God. It was as if we thought the "God" word had been prohibited, and we were suddenly convicted to reclaim it.

One Monday evening when I came home from a YFC meeting, something very eerie happened. I came into the house and heard a small "plink" on the wood floor. I bent down to see what had fallen. It was my cross that I never take off. I grabbed at my throat—the chain was still there. Chills ran down my arms as I remembered a few months earlier the same thing had happened. At that time, I had examined the pendant carefully to see if the bail needed to be welded by a jeweler. To my surprise, there was no break in the link. I remember thinking it was odd, but then forgot about the incident. Now, six months later, the same cross had fallen again. How had it fallen from its chain? I stood holding the cross in my hand, stunned and unsettled. Kellie had observed the whole thing, and was frightened, thinking it might be a bad omen.

"I don't think so," I said as I stuck a pencil point into the bail to see if the pressure would pry it open at a weakened spot. The gold held firm. I was getting a magnifying glass as Bruce, all business, was telling me there must be a logical explanation. I gave him the cross, the chain from my neck, and the magnifying glass to investigate for himself. He never offered an explanation, though being a scientist, he knew there must be one.

Bruce and I have different kinds of brains. He always answers my questions gently, as though I am a small, simple-minded child. My naivety causes him to put his arm around me and shake his head sometimes, like when I am amazed that big, heavy airplanes can actually get off the ground and that someone was smart enough to conceive of telephones, and televisions, and computers, inventions that if left to people with *my* kind of brain, would never have made it *to*, and definitively not *off*, the drawing board! CDs really boggle my mind—how anyone could have imagined that it was possible to put all that information, even moving pictures and sound, on a flat, hard disc less than five inches in diameter is beyond me!

I cannot understand the technology I see every day around me, but I know it's real. Bruce knew it was impossible for my cross to fall, yet a soldered ring had fallen from a fastened chain. I was well aware he was unimpressed with the mystery of my cross, not because he couldn't believe in the supernatural, but because he was not privy to the assembling pieces of an enormous, invisible puzzle. He wasn't looking for mystical revelations from God, because I had not shared that *I* had experienced mystical revelations from God!

I didn't wear my cross for the next couple of days, afraid that it might fall off, and I wouldn't hear it when it fell. Both times the cross fell, I was at home where it hit the wood floor instead of rugs which cover the majority of my floors. I believed there was a message in my cross. Finally I put it back on, sure that the only way it could have fallen off was God trying to get my attention. He had it now, and I felt that my cross was safe to wear. It has never fallen off since. I still don't understand why my cross fell away from its chain. Maybe it was just for the experience of a supernatural phenomenon. Later, when additional puzzle pieces revealed more details of God's plan, I wanted to believe the messages were my imagination. At those moments, I remembered the antics of my cross as a concrete, miraculous gift from God, actual occurrences that were not created by my imagination.

Meanwhile, despite my mini-assignments, the ominous adoption idea loomed on the periphery of my daily life. Our *Experiencing God* study revealed that if I had an obedience problem, I had a love problem. I had to ask myself, did I love God with all my heart, mind, body and soul? Did I love God more than I loved my family or myself? These were dangerous questions, because simply asking them required that I answer them, and I already knew the answers were no.

The book warned "God's ways and thoughts are so different from ours they will often sound wrong or crazy." They were definitely sounding wrong *and* crazy to me. Why wouldn't the thoughts of adoption just fade away? I was determined to erase them from my thoughts, but they always crept stealthily back into the fringes of my consciousness.

"God," I finally cried out, "This would change my whole life."

The thought that involuntarily bounced right back to me was, *"Think of how it would change his life."*

This was no James Earl Jones-sized voice; it was just a thought, but it came out of nowhere.

His life. . . *his* life?

This mental "conversation" coincided with the chapter in *Experiencing God* that boiled down to: if God tells me to do something, I have to do it. He's God. He has a right to tell me what to do. I was ready to stop reading this annoying book! I was afraid to read my daily lessons, worried that God would use the reading to make me feel guilty, again.

Although I had always been a comatose sleeper, the topic I struggled to ignore all of my waking hours began to yank me from sound sleep about 2 a.m. every night. I had an overwhelming feeling that I should go downstairs, read the Bible and pray. Most nights I would just lie there and cry, begging God not to make me get out of my warm, comfortable bed and cope with such a worrisome topic as adoption. My repugnance to the adoption idea and my fear of the consequences of disobedience were becoming consuming.

Bruce was aware of my sleepless nights, and my inconsolable doldrums, but he was powerless to help me. He was gentle when dealing with me, but never asked the questions that I could read on his worried face. He was completely in the dark about the reason behind my internal turmoil, and I couldn't ease his mind by telling him it was nothing. I couldn't talk about it.

Then one morning, another disturbing message nagged at me from a small article in the morning newspaper.

"Is that you, God?" I asked, fearful.

A local adoption agency was recruiting host families for visiting Russian orphans. My shoulders slumped.

"Please no God!" I said aloud.

The article explained that the children were scheduled to come for a week-long visit in August. The Cherry Orchard Program, as it was called, was based on an Anton Chekhov play, and the idea that to have worldwide peace, one must begin in one's own backyard. I started reading with the same apprehension the idea of adoption always evoked in me.

"If you have ever considered adopting an older child, you don't want to miss this informational meeting," the article coaxed.

With a defiance that scared me, I closed the newspaper without finishing the article. I wasn't going to do it. I wasn't going to adopt, and that was final. God had given me other assignments, and I was being obedient to those callings. God could not possibly understand how much distress the idea of adoption caused me. I was going to pass on this one.

And that thought scared me even more. Now I was faced with an excruciatingly sick feeling that I was going to be miserable if I did adopt, and equally wretched if I didn't.

My next lesson from *Experiencing God* revealed "obedience is costly, to me and to those around me." Adoption imposed a cost I was unwilling to pay. It would change the entire dynamics of my happy home. Everything would be altered; every one of us would have a price to pay. Heather, Kellie, and Taylor could not imagine all the sacrifices that would be required of them. Bruce was obviously not getting these same messages from God; therefore, he would surely be skeptical. If he came to me with the same dilemma, if God had spoken to him instead of me, I would think he was out of his mind! And being a reluctant caregiver to a child I never wanted in the first place might cause me to be resentful. I did not want to grow old and bitter.

But Henry Blackaby continued; "if God speaks to me and I hear but do not respond, a time could come when I will not hear His voice. Disobedience can lead to a famine of hearing the words of the Lord." Although I didn't want to hear God's voice about *adoption*, it terrified me to think about being separated from God forever. Until this study, I was unaware that I could even have such a relationship with God. Now that I had felt God speak to my heart, how could I dismiss Him.

My restless nights continued. God, would I ever be able to sleep again? One night I finally got up after God nagged me relentlessly. I got my Bible, prayed on my knees for God to speak to me, and opened it up to Psalms 127:3-5. (CEV)

> "Children are a blessing and a gift from the Lord.
> Having a lot of children to take care of you in your
> old age is like a warrior with a lot of arrows. The
> more you have, the better off you will be, because
> they will protect you when your enemies attack with
> arguments."

It was an odd translation in this new Bible I was reading, but that is exactly what it said. And, besides, we had all the arrows we needed, thank you very much!

I didn't want to see anything about children in the inspired scriptures, but I could not deny God was speaking to me.

I continued with the next chapter:

> "The lord will bless you if you respect him and obey
> his laws. Your fields will produce, and you will be
> happy and all will go well. Your wife will be as
> fruitful as a grapevine, and just as an olive tree is
> rich with olives, your home will be rich with healthy

children. That is how the Lord will bless everyone
who respects him." Psalm 128:1-4 (CEV)

Oh dear!

What would my family say to this preposterous idea? They had
no warning, no insight, no messages from God. Perhaps I should
talk to them about it, and then I could finally put the idea to rest.
Surely they would put their collective feet down and come up with
hundreds of reasons why we shouldn't listen to God.

I had not wanted to talk to anyone about the persistent prodding
to adopt. If someone had come to me and said, "God is telling me
to adopt an orphan," I would say . . . well, I wouldn't know exactly
what to say to a crazy person. But, if the person seemed reasonable
and lucid, I might say, "If *God* is telling you to do it, then I guess
you have to do it!"

I did not know in which camp I belonged—the crazy or the
sane!

How could I say I felt *God* was calling me to adopt, and then
refuse to comply? I remained silent hoping no one would have to
judge my sanity or my character.

Chapter Eight

"Don't you see that children
are God's best gift?"

Psalm 127:3 (MSG)

When Heather was born in October, 1981, I could not have been prepared for the gush of devotion I instantly felt for this beautiful, pink, grunting, little parasite! I thought that I would have to wait a while before she had a personality, but the adoration was immediate and intense. So was the fear that something would happen to her. Now that I was a mother, how would I ever live without my baby? All day I marveled at her perfect rosebud mouth, her tiny chest rising and falling, her wax-like skin so translucent that I could study the blood traveling through the blue veins just below the surface. Her miniature hands with flawlessly manicured nails. Every part of her was a miracle. I was totally fixated on my new baby. A neglected cat who had once been a pampered pet moped around in depression. Bruce generously took second place to this new object of my affection and devotion. Who knew that motherhood could be so joyfully consuming? Certainly not me!

When Bruce came home in the evenings, his face was enormous compared to the tiny round head, fuzzy with colorless hair that I had studied all day. I was sure that Heather would be an only child—how could I ever love another child this much? I knew that I could not divide my affection with another little stranger. But what if something happened to my new baby? Not that another child could take her place, but the thought of being childless was now unbearable!

When Heather was two, we discovered that we were expecting again. As soon as Kellie was born in April of 1984, the burst of love that took my breath away came flooding back. My love wasn't divided in half; I suddenly had twice as much. I left a full-time job that I had returned to when Heather was ten months old, feeling blessed to be a stay-at-home mom. "One is like none, and two is like ten," a wise southern relative told me when Kellie was born. It wasn't long before I understood that she meant! Laundry would mildew in the washer before I remembered to move it to the dryer. Some days, my only lunch was crusts from peanut butter and jelly sandwiches and crumb-filled milk from smudgy, plastic cups. Bruce would return home from work to find the house strewn with toys and no dinner on the table. I had loved my job at National Geographic in downtown Washington, D.C., but I adored staying home with my babies. Life was so blissful and comfortable, if not clean and tidy! I found a poem that became my mantra and proudly displayed it on the refrigerator door:

HOUSEWORK CAN WAIT

Come in but don't expect to find
All dishes done, all floors a shine.
Observe the crumpled rug.
The toys galore,
The smudgy fingerprinted door.
The little ones we shelter here
Don't thrive on spotless atmosphere.
They're more inclined to disarray
And carefree, even messy play!

Their needs are great,
Their patience small.
All day, I'm at their beck and call.
It's Mommy come, Mommy see!"
Wiggly worms and red scraped knee.
Painted pictures, blocks piled high,
My floors, unshined,
The days go by.
Some future day they'll flee this nest
And I at last will have a rest!
Now you tell me which matters more, A happy child
Or a polished floor?

Author Unknown

Heather and Kellie, 1986

I cried when Heather boarded the towering yellow bus that carried her out of the snug cocoon of our home and off to kindergarten. She was ready. When Kellie was four, I began to dread the pangs that I knew were inevitable when she too would board the bus the next year. My babies were leaving the nest!

I started to talk to Bruce about another baby. We had a friend who had recently delivered a baby boy, so any negative resolve he felt was weakened by watching me hold and smell a new baby. Taylor was born in May of 1989, the spring before Kellie started kindergarten. Heather was in second grade. The ecstasy of motherhood began anew. It was easier this time; I was more relaxed. I knew that every stage he went through, good and bad, would be too brief, and I wanted to enjoy every moment. He was an adored little boy. Kellie was a doting little mother. Heather was helpful when she was available, but, at seven, she was distracted by friends and school. Nothing held a greater appeal to Kellie than holding that baby, and as he grew, playing with him gently and lovingly. They were always devoted playmates, even though five years separated them.

I didn't know how sweet little boys could be. Taylor was quite secure knowing that he was loved. Until the age of six, he told people he wanted to be a "mom" when he grew up. He could tell I had a job that anyone would love. As soon as Taylor neared kindergarten age, I again started to have the "empty nest" pangs. This time I ignored them!

Not everyone wants to, or should be, a mother. But I knew that my life would not have been fulfilling and fun if we had never had kids. They gave me a purpose and joy that no career ever could have matched. I have treasured and enjoyed my children more than anyone else I know. My family has been my favorite blessing. I am also thankful Bruce is the one who shared the role of parenting with me.

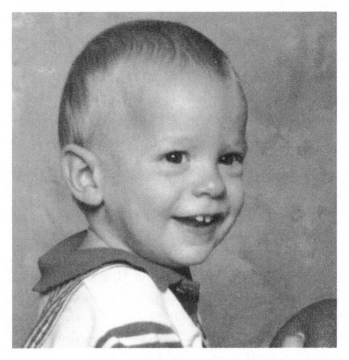

Taylor, 1990

From the time my children were little, I have always been in the habit of spending fifteen or twenty minutes with each child before bedtime. This was a time I cherished. Taylor would be first, because he was the youngest, and his bedtime was the earliest. I would lie beside him in his bed, read him books, and tell him the sweet stuff of life: how I was glad he was my little boy, that he was my favorite boy in the whole world. He was a boy who, by his eleventh birthday, still sat on my lap and wouldn't go to bed without our nightly ritual. When he was in kindergarten, he came home one day and announced that he was a big boy, and didn't want to say the love words anymore. I was heartbroken but knew him well enough to know he didn't know what that would mean. I said okay, and every time I started to say sweet things to him, I would stop myself and say, "Oh, I forgot that we are not saying those words anymore."

He changed his mind the same day as his announcement. Even at eleven, he was a boy who loved being loved. And he was a kind, tender-hearted boy. I have always told my children stories of the world's less fortunate, in hopes of instilling compassion in them, and to help them think beyond themselves. I wanted them to be grateful for the life into which they had been born. Once, after I shared a tragic story about a homeless child, I asked Taylor "Do you know why I tell you these sad stories?"

His earnest little face was attentive as he guessed at the right answer, "To make us cry?"

"No," I explained, "to help you understand how blessed you are."

With the thought of adoption hanging over my head like an ax, he seemed even more precious to me. He had been my baby for eleven years. He would not relinquish that coveted position easily. One night when I was putting him to bed, I felt particularly tender toward him. My secret that I had been unable to tell anyone for two tortuous months was about to find a small voice.

I began by telling him the same kind of story that made him want to cry, this time about the many children in the world who didn't have families like ours to love them. He groaned at the painful thought. The empathy of the little fellow encouraged me to continue.

I casually mentioned that I felt that God might want to add one of those unfortunate children to our family. We had so much love, we had enough to share with someone who had no one. I chose my words carefully, saying "our family" instead of "me" because I wanted him to feel involved. Maybe I was testing the waters by including the child who would be most affected by any action we would take regarding adoption.

His expression did not change.

After a moment, he said, "You know Mom, I never told you, but I always wanted a little brother." This was a response that only halfway surprised me; he was a wise old soul in a little boy's body.

I felt euphoric. If we had to bear this inconceivable burden, maybe Taylor would be okay. It would be harder than he could imagine now, than any of us could imagine, but God had gotten to him too.

I reread my lesson that night after the kids were in bed. *Experiencing God* promised me that God will not give me an assignment if He is not willing to equip me to do it.

Almost daily, Taylor would want to talk about this unknown child who needed us. He would encourage me to move forward. I began to regret that I had mentioned it to him. Now I felt more pressure to investigate the options. Sometimes I minimized the possibility that we would actually adopt. I reverted to my stories about generic homeless children, telling him we would *pray* for them. Bruce was still not privy to the information about those needy children, or a particular needy child. Taylor didn't like that I was wavering.

"Maybe God wants to use our family. Maybe after we adopt, other people will see us and want to adopt too," he said gently to me.

I was touched by his sweet naivety, but I knew better than he could understand what would be sacrificed for this mission.

"Mom," he tried a different path. "Remember when you kept Linnie." Of course I did. She and Taylor were about one and a half when Carol, a neighbor, needed a babysitter four days a week. I volunteered. It would be a playmate for Tay and money for me. I smiled to think about those lovely times.

My therapist son continued, "She was practically a stranger when she started coming, and then you loved her like the rest of us." I smiled again, pleased that his memory of that time had been as pleasant as my own. These two children had grown up together. I kept her until she was five when her family moved out of our neighborhood to another part of our community. We continue to attend the same church and see Linnie, now "Linnet," regularly. Taylor continued to remind me of other children who had entered my life and left a lasting impression of love. In the summer of 1997, we had hosted a couple of teenage French boys who were part of an exchange program. They only stayed with us for a week, but we had so much fun. I cried as I hugged them goodbye as they boarded the bus that would carry them to the airport and out of our lives forever.

The year after the French kids visited, Heather, Kellie, and I joined a budget excursion with Kellie's middle school social studies teacher to Italy and France. I was one of ten adults chaperoning, and I had accepted the fact that my girls might want to be on their own with the other teenagers and not spend much time with me. But to the contrary, they switched rooms so we three could stay together, and the second night, we had two girls ask to sleep on our floor. A few days into the trip, I felt like the Pied Piper with most of the group following me around Rome, Florence, and Nice. They really did need a "mom" in charge, even if it wasn't their own. I was addressed as "Mom" by eight kids, in addition to my own. I enjoyed their company, and they allowed me to sit with them at meals instead of banishing me to the tables of the other adults. As we separated at the airport back in the states, birth mothers watched me suspiciously as their kids hugged me and called me "Mom."

And now there was the substituting. Taylor was observing me getting attached to kids at school. Every day I would come home with a story and a new name to share. My family could tell I loved my job, and it wasn't the $70 per day, or the work; it was the students.

"This is just the next logical step," his coaxing was calming. "If God tells you to do something, you have to do it." The hair at the back of my neck stood on end as I realized that Taylor's words were the same ones that Henry Blackaby used in *Experiencing God*.

I felt like I should be laid out on his couch, waiting for him to tell me our session was over, and I could pay on the way out! I marveled at the wisdom of this dear eleven-year-old, and more so, the cleverness of God who used this child whom I adored with every cell in my body, who I still babied because he was, after all, my baby!

The Sunday after my counseling session with Taylor, I went to church by myself. Bruce was already there because he had attended the men's group breakfast. I had walked out of the house as Taylor and Kellie were getting ready. They had dilly-dallied and were not ready when it was time to go, so I left them. They knew there would be trouble later when I returned home. That only happened that one time!

I sat alone in my usual pew. As we were singing the opening songs, I watched as Linnie, the same Linnie who I had babysat years earlier, crossed in front of the altar and headed down my aisle. I wondered what she was up to until she asked the woman at the end of my pew to excuse her. She came and sat beside me. She had never done that before. As we sang "Our God is an Awesome God," Taylor's words resounded in my head: "Linnie came to you as a stranger and you learned to love her like the rest of us." I put my arm around her shoulder, and we continued to sing as tears rolled down my smiling face. After the service, I told Carol I would tell her someday how God had used her daughter to speak to me. Carol seemed curious, but that was the only clue that I was ready to share.

Again I would remember Henry Blackaby's and Taylor's words, "If God tells you to do something, you have to do it." I knew they were right. Months later, when the adoption was imminent, Taylor confessed that the thought had, in fact, never crossed his mind about always wanting a little brother.

"But isn't it interesting that you said it!" I told him. He smiled, understanding his impact on my decision.

Talking to the girls about God's nudging and the possibility of adopting a boy would be easier. Their lives would not be so rearranged by an addition to the family. Heather was already away at college. Kellie, who loved babies and children, was already preparing for college too. I knew enough to know that adoptions don't happen overnight, so, by the time he arrived, whoever "he" was, Kellie would only have a short time before she left for college too.

Referring to adoption in hypothetical terms, I talked to them separately, stressing the idea as still a "remote possibility." I didn't reveal particulars, like the persistent Russian theme, or that it seemed that we were destined to adopt an older child. They both responded positively to my casual statement that I felt God wanted us to adopt. They surprised me with their open hearts and willingness to accept the idea.

Kellie, my middle child who never even went through the terrible twos, was at sixteen, still steady as a rock. As a toddler, she would gently, almost playfully push her limits, quickly backing down when she reached them.

"Let's be happy!" she would say, smiling in my face if she thought I was angry or upset. She was the most pleasant of children. A highly imaginative three year old, she liked to take her snacks from a bowl on the floor when she was pretending to be a puppy. When she was a pony, she whinnied through the grocery store, pawing the air with her front hooves as she reared up, humiliating her mature, five-and–a-half-year-old sister.

"Can't you make her stop?" Heather would impatiently plead, and then walk ahead like she didn't know the galloping half-girl with the bouncing golden mane and the permissive mother who allowed such outrageous behavior in public!

At three, Kellie once drew on her bedspread with a permanent marker. I ranted and raved, partly because I wanted to make an impression on her, but mostly because I was out of control with anger and frustration. I *loved* that spread, and we couldn't afford to replace it. She patiently waited for me to stop to take a breath. When I paused to get a reaction from her and gauge my effectiveness, she calmly said, without ever looking at me, "Let's pretend you're a baby, and you can't talk." I walked out of the room, unable to say another word, amused, but also ashamed that I could be so angry about such a trivial thing. She never again drew on her bedspread, or anything else inappropriate, but draw she did. Kellie's artistic abilities were clear to me by the time she was three. She and Heather both had exceptional gifts for drawing. As early as two and a half, their stick figures had fingers and toes, eight or nine on each hand and foot! I was a proud mom! As far as the bedspread, Kellie was taking a leap to textile design, I suppose.

This middle-child diplomat was thrilled by the idea of adopting an orphan. Her enthusiasm was more than I had desired. She would love to share her affections with a needy child. I tried to tone down her excitement, again, emphasizing that the idea of adopting was probably just a passing thought. But Kellie was not to be dissuaded. Her initial comment was the biggest compliment she could have given me as a mother. "I think anyone would be lucky to be a part of our family."

God had gotten to her too.

When I talked to Heather, who was away at school most of the time now, I framed our conversation in the context of a local family's example. The Pucinos had adopted three of their foster children last year, adding to their three biological kids. How would Heather feel if that were her family? Heather admired the Pucinos for what they were doing. It didn't' hurt that they were a loved and admired family in the larger community. The kids were popular at school. They made it seem so "cool" to have adopted younger siblings.

Heather was always a serious little girl. When she was a three-year-old, I was trying to describe our purchase in three-year-old language: It was a "box to put on the top of the television so we could watch any movie we wanted to, any time we liked." She stared off with a confused look, a frown on her impish little face. Then she asked, "You mean kinda like a VCR?"

"Uh, yeah, something like that," I answered stupidly.

When she went to college, I was pleased to see her occasionally erupt into bouts of silliness that I thought she had missed as a child. Her well-respected high school English teacher, Ms. Evans, had bequeathed to Heather in the Senior "Last Will and Testament" in the school newspaper "a tolerance for nonsense." She had none. Most of the time, this was a good thing. She took school work very seriously, but she had little patience with students who goofed off or otherwise acted like the teenagers they were. I knew she would take our mission seriously. She came to me one day during one of her weekends at home and said the child could have her room. I was touched by her charity, but I reminded her that an adoption was something I had only barely considered. But she was thinking about it and already accepting the possibility, eager to be generous about her role in the assignment. This was the same young lady who, when she left for college a year earlier, had told us all, in succinct language that her room was off limits! I sometimes felt that she was the boss of all of us. But it seemed that God had softened her heart too about the possibility of adoption.

Certainly no decision had been made concerning adoption, but the nudges were difficult to ignore. I was starting to get a little nervous about the shrouded secrecy with the kids. I had disclosed nothing to Bruce about the reason for my turmoil of the last few months. I had fervently hoped and wrongly assumed that the specter of adoption would vanish before I ever had to explain the vague feelings and weird incidents that had led me to this conclusion. They sounded unreasonable even to me. I was sure the children would nix the idea before I ever had to present it to their rational father. The whole proposition sounded ludicrous, and there was no reason to worry him for nothing. But the puzzle was fitting together even without my cooperation. It was clear I would soon need to have a serious discussion with my husband. It seemed absurd I had mentioned it to my children, as only a hypothetical, passing thought, but had not been able to approach my husband who I trusted with my heart.

Although all three children agreed we should not mention a possible, though still remote, adoption to anyone because we were just "considering" it, there were little leaks. A secretary at school asked me one day if we were planning to adopt. A neighbor asked me if it were true. I gave vague answers and later spoke to the children about our secret. This was news too exciting to hide! I knew I needed to tell Bruce soon. Still it was hard to broach the subject. I could put it off another week, only because of everyone's distractions during spring break.

We went to North Carolina for the week before Easter to visit Mother and my sister Weegie. One day, when the kids and Bruce were occupied elsewhere, I sat at the kitchen table where years earlier, many secrets had been disclosed. As a young school girl, I had a rare relationship with my mother. Unlike many of my friends, I believed my mother knew what she was talking about when she advised me about relationships with friends, boys and girls. I trusted her counsel and enjoyed telling her most of my secrets.

I longed to be a school girl again and have my mother give me advice that I knew I could trust. I told her about the *Experiencing God* book and my note to the middle school student that had set off a chain reaction that, incredibly, forced me to consider adopting a child, as reluctant as I continued to be. I told her about my cross falling off and all the signs that pointed me in the direction of adopting an older Russian boy. As I was sharing these experiences, I thought they sounded ludicrous. Had this whole thing been my imagination? But Mother listened intently. She was touched to hear the story, and she was impressed that I had been nudged to such a noble call.

"I always wanted to do something like that when I was younger. To help an innocent child would be the greatest reward," she encouraged.

Okay, all three of my children thought this adoption plan was a good idea, and my mother agreed. I was uncertain whether I was pleased about her support. Maybe I wanted my mother to remind me how full my hands were already with the three kids I had.

Wouldn't she worry that I had taken on too much or be troubled by the unknown variables of a possibly damaged child?

Weegie and I visited my ninety-year-old grandmother who lived three hours away. My sister drove as I talked on and on to my captive audience about the circumstances that had forced me to believe that God wanted me to adopt. My sister offered me no advice; she neither tried to discourage me, nor encouraged me. She agreed that my story was incredible, that it was frightening to be confronted with an "assignment" from God of such magnitude. She interpreted clues the same way I did.

When we returned to Maryland, Gretta, my *Experiencing God* partner, announced in our Sunday school class that she and her fourteen-year-old daughter were moving to West Virginia. We were all stunned because Gretta had a lucrative job with the government, and her daughter was going to be starting high school in the fall. They seemed happy where they were. Gretta had not mentioned anything to me about this plan during our study evenings, but I had been silent as well about what God was asking me to do. She explained that when she first felt the nudging to move, she tried to ignore it. She believed that God was urging her to relocate to West Virginia and start a music ministry at a new church. She did not want to do it. Maryland had always been her home. She struggled for weeks feeling God pulling her in a direction that she was not willing to go. Her story sounded frighteningly familiar. We both had been afraid to talk about the direction in which God was nudging us, because we had both read in *Experiencing God* that if God tells you to do something, you have to do it. We didn't want to be held accountable for our disobedience.

God is persistent.

Finally, one morning Gretta was reading her morning devotional calendar. The words she read shocked her. "If you have to sell your house and move to be obedient to God, do it." She talked to her daughter, who was thrilled with the idea of a new adventure and a fresh start. The single mother put her house on the market, and it sold to the first couple to come through, in a market that had been slow. I was stunned that God had worked on Gretta in such a similar way as me. As she enthusiastically related God's miracles in revealing to her the mission that He planned for her, and the smooth execution of that plan, I was silent and ashamed that my own commission was still a guarded secret.

Soon afterwards, Bruce and I went out to eat at a local restaurant with the gift certificate that was part of my $102 refund from God months earlier. Though it was an appropriate opportunity, I hadn't intended to tell him of these "nudgings" while we were at a restaurant. I had thought I would tell him in the solitude and safety of home. But I started talking about the *Experiencing God* book and how much I had been enlightened. I told him about the $100 I had given to the woman at school, and the "payback." Then without any preparation, or introduction, with no planning or rehearsal, I jumped in.

"And I feel like we are supposed to adopt a Russian orphan," I confessed more casually than I might have said, "I'm changing my hair color." A piece of romaine lettuce dangled from my fork as I watched to assess his reaction.

There really wasn't much of a reaction. Bruce had lived with me for twenty-three years. Not much surprised him anymore. He had survived many of my crazy ideas. This too would pass. He said something about as supportive as "that's interesting." I knew he didn't take me seriously. I think I wanted him to look at me like I had two heads and say something like "you're crazy, we can't do that," to which I was eager to finally be a submissive wife and respond, "okay, whatever you say, you're the boss."

Several times in the following weeks I reminded him that I was completely serious. He said he would have to think about it. I knew that was fair. I had been thinking about it for six months!

Then he did something totally out of character—he told people about it. Suddenly members of the United Methodist Men and the guy in Bruce's carpool were privy to my much-guarded secret. I had told Taylor, then Kellie, then Heather, asking each of them not to tell anyone until we decided for sure. When I told Bruce, I was sure he wouldn't mention it to a sole. Most men don't want other men to know about their wives' mental lapses. Bruce doesn't like humiliation any more than the next guy; I thought my secret was safe with him!

I didn't want to tell *anyone*. Some people would think I was crazy, just because I said *God* was telling me to do it. The blank looks and the cynicism would cause awkwardness for everyone. I am a prideful person; I didn't want people to cross the street to avoid contact with me. But the main reason I did not want to tell others was, if I said that *God* was leading me to adopt an older Russian child, I would have to *do* it. I believed then, and still believe, that if God tells me to do something, I have to do it. God is the giver of life and all its blessings, and He has the right to tell me what to do.

But, and there was always a "but," I was still waiting to make sure that adoption was *actually* what He was asking of me.

When Bruce began blabbing my secret, I had to go behind him and reiterate that we were just exploring the possibility. I talked to Cindy, my friend of ten years and Sunday school teacher. From her I got only support, no skepticism or awkwardness. She allowed herself to be a sounding board. She was familiar in the ways that God worked. I didn't want to make any announcements in Sunday school class where all doubtful eyes would be on me. I feared that I would be too emotional. I would just let Bruce's rumors spread, and gradually I would fill in the blanks, reminding everyone that we were just thinking about it. That was my disclosure of choice. As people heard about our "plans," my church family circled the wagons to lift us up in support and protection. Some offered more practical advice: one offered to let us keep his two-year-old for a while. That would surely cure us of wanting any more children!

Chapter Nine

*"Religion that God our Father accepts
as pure and faultless is this: to look after
orphans and widows in their distress."*

James 1:27a (NIV)

One morning when I was reading the newspaper, there was a feature article about Big Brothers and Big Sisters. I suddenly read with intense interest. Maybe God intended for me to see this article. Maybe this is what He wanted me to do. I hung on to the idea with eager hope. I could be an enthusiastic Big Sister. This "assignment" would be costly in terms of my time, and it would impact a child's life, but my life would not be totally rearranged permanently. I could do this. I called for an application that same day, thankful I hadn't made any commitments to adoption. This is probably what God was trying to tell me all along. Maybe my persistent fear meant adoption was never what He meant. How silly I had been!

A week later, another article featured foster parenting. My heart sank a little. Maybe this was what God wanted me to do. This would require a lot more than being a Big Sister, bringing a child into my home to rescue him from tragic situation. I wouldn't really have to *love* the child, but I could be compassionate, consistent, and dependable. Isn't this what a disadvantaged child needed most?

These assignments were set up to be temporary—I wouldn't want the child to get too attached to us, so if he had to go back to his family, it would be less painful for all of us.

I liked the temporary part. I thought I could be a foster parent maybe, if that is what God asked of me. Either of these options was within my realm of capability and comfort. I called for an application. It was June, and they told me the next training session would be in August. Perfect! That gave me some time for this whole cloud of irresolution to dissipate—I just wanted my life back, my comfortable, uncomplicated life, without any confusing assignments and additional children under our roof.

Because I had months to consider foster care, I shelved the thought of it. I did complete the Big Sister application. I sent out the references to be completed by my friends; I met with the woman in charge; I had a background check; the coordinator came out to my house for a home study; and then I waited. Although the Frederick County director of Big Brothers/Big Sisters had told me there was a waiting list of forty girls, I heard nothing for three months. I was slightly relieved. This hadn't been my idea.

Or had it?

I threw myself into anything that might get me off the hook of bringing a needy child into my home forever. Forever was a long time, and I was finding the prospect impossible to commit to. Forever was for the rest of my life. I wasn't prepared to lose my life. I was unwilling to start over with another child who possibly had enough rejection in his life to cause problems in mine. I was not equipped to handle deeply buried psychological ailments. And how could I ever love another child as I love Heather, Kellie, and Taylor? I loved the kids at school and at YFC, but not as a mother loves her own child. Were other adoptive mothers capable of truly loving their adopted children? I couldn't imagine that *I* could. That should be enough of a reason not to do it—I was not *qualified* to adopt.

I had heard of a family who had adopted a girl from Russia with the best intentions, only to discover they did not bond and could not cope with the disturbed child. They had relinquished her to Social Services, where she was eventually placed with another family. The prospect that I might later reject a child who I so clearly felt that God had led me to adopt was a regret I knew I could not live with. Better not to adopt in the first place!

Forgive me God. I just would *not* do it.

I became a fill-in counselor for the junior high youth group at church on Sunday nights, on an as-needed basis. I couldn't commit myself fully because of my volunteer work with Youth for Christ. I had all kinds of ideas, all sorts of jobs I could do for God. Certainly one or all of these missions would please, or at least appease, God. I waited for the peace I longed for. It eluded me. Looking back over my *Experiencing God* book, I came across the lesson where I had highlighted a passage warning me not to try to do things for God but rather to wait for God to tell me what He wanted me to do for Him.

Nag, nag, nag.

I was beginning to hate that book!

I continued to hear about the Russian orphans on the radio. I didn't listen long enough to understand the message. Once I heard "Russian orphans," I changed stations.

Then one morning a dreadful thing happened. The group of orphans from Russia I had refused to read about months ago was in the newspaper. Their trip was documented with pictures of five children, ages five to seven, smiling gleefully. I studied the happy faces. I wondered if one of these motherless children was supposed to be mine.

The sleepless nights resumed. God had something to tell me, whether or not I wanted to listen. I could fight it, and I had certainly tried, but I was learning that obstinate refusal did not work. I wanted my sleep, and I wanted some peace. I got up one night when summoned and got my Bible. I would try it His way, but not quite, because I was determined to miss the Old Testament and the wrath of God parts. God wrestled control back from we when He had me open to James 1:26–27 (GNT):

"Do any of you think you are religious? If you do not control your tongue, your religion is worthless and you deceive yourself."

That might have been my problem sometimes, but not in this case, so I continued, at great risk.

"What God the Father considers to be pure and genuine religion is this: to take care of orphans and widows in their suffering and to keep oneself from being corrupted by the world."

I groaned, feeling like I had been kicked in the gut. Tears of hopeless dread rolled down my cheeks. I thanked God for His word, even if I didn't want to hear it.

Defeated, I drug a tired body and a heavy heart back upstairs to my room. I slipped into bed, turning my back to Bruce. My worried husband rolled over and patted my arm.

"I love you," he whispered.

"I'm glad. I love you too," my weak voice managed through my broken breaths.

I called the adoption agency the next morning to ask about the children. Were any of them going back to Russia? I thought if the children were going to be adopted, they would be allowed to stay in the country. Sharon, a kind voice on the other end of the phone, explained they all were required to return to Russia. If their hosts wanted to adopt them, they would have to travel to Russia and adopt them in Russian courts. That seemed unfortunate to me since they were already here. I asked about one small boy, the one with the biggest smile, with dark curly hair. He was adorable. But according to Sharon, his host family had decided to adopt him even before he arrived.

She gave me some general information. The cost shocked me: $16,000—as much as a car that we so badly needed. I immediately felt guilty for comparing a car to a child's life. But it was so much more than I had expected. I would learn later that was only the partial "bill."

And what about the costs to my family that I could not even begin to calculate? Once again Henry Blackaby's words came back to me: "Joining God requires major adjustments ... How I respond to God's invitation reveals what I believe about God—can He do what He says He will do? ... Following God's will always requires faith, action and adjustments that are costly to me and to those around me."

God had me in His grip.

Chapter Ten

"Coincidences are spiritual puns."

G. K. Chesterton

By August, I was finally ready to go on the Walk to Emmaus so many in our church family had attended. Our friends had urged us for two years to attend the three day spiritual retreat in nearby West Virginia. One week during Sunday school, the class was talking about the upcoming weekend's "pilgrims," as those attending were called. Someone asked us again when we were going. I confessed I had picked up an application. Someone else pulled out another application from a notebook and gave it to Bruce. They waited while we each filled one out and then whisked them off as if we might change our minds if given time for second thoughts. Within a couple of weeks, it was confirmed: Bruce would attend the men's weekend in September, and I was scheduled for the women's weekend in October.

People didn't talk about the particulars experienced on their given weekend. The consensus was that the event was awesome, and when one went, that weekend was *the* weekend he or she was supposed to be there. A person's Emmaus experience was defined by God, and His intention was always specific.

During Bruce's weekend, God didn't speak to him about

adoption, but it was a faith-building experience for my husband. He returned home aglow after his September retreat. I asked about his experience, and though I wanted details, his answers were vague: "awesome," "wonderful," and "amazing." People he had not seen or thought of in years were surprisingly in attendance during his weekend. He had felt the love of God. We had come a long way spiritually in the past several months. His weekend was an affirmation of God's intimate involvement in his life.

When my opportunity came, my expectations were high. As in the spring when I had participated in the *Experiencing God* study, I had that magical, anticipatory feeling again. I felt like God-size things were about to happen.

I suffer from a delusion of self-importance. I was sure that my family could not endure without me for the three days I would be away. I had thought that was my reason for not going earlier. But the real reason was that God was waiting for me to go at precisely the right time.

The third Thursday evening in October, we pilgrims, about twenty-four in all, arrived. We ate together and played "ice breaking" games to get acquainted. When we were dismissed for bed, we were instructed not to talk to anyone until after communion Friday morning. It was a little awkward passing three smiling, yet unfamiliar roommates in the bathroom without speaking. Everyone turned in early because there was little else to do. We were awakened early for communion. Our watches had been confiscated (this was a time before everyone had cell phones), so our concept of time was off. Still I could tell by the morning light that it was early. Again we were silent as we made our way to the make-shift chapel. As one of the first to enter the side door of the small, simple room, I became acutely aware that where I sat would have considerable importance. I moved straight to the second row from the front and sat on the seat beside the aisle. After receiving Holy Communion, I returned to my seat and prayed for discernment. The adoption was still very much a part of my daily prayers and a continuing source of anguish. A sad gnawing at my heart never went away. I was praying more for God to release me from the assignment than to prepare me for it. I opened my eyes after another one of my selfish prayers, just as a woman was passing me at my seat on the aisle. I became alert, and something made me turn and watch her return to her seat. As she entered the last row and turned to face the front to sit down, I saw it: on the front of her shirt was printed "Faith is adopting an orphan."

I stared, turned backwards in my seat, unable to believe God's boldness. His presence was so real to me. There was almost an *electricity* surrounding me. The sick feeling that had become so familiar whenever the word "adoption" intruded on my mind was replaced by a peace I had never imagined before. This suddenly seemed like, not only something that I could do, but something that I was in partnership with God about.

When we moved into our table groups of six, with whom we would remain for the rest of the weekend, I waited as each woman in turn gave a little information about herself, and when it was my turn, I started babbling about the past seven months and communion and the shirt. I cried. No, I gushed.

When I had finished, one older woman spoke sweetly and wisely, "I adopted an older child twenty-five years ago."

Then another woman about my age, instinctively added, "And I was adopted as an older child."

This truly was my weekend to be there.

The woman in the shirt? I only saw her one other time, when I searched for her. A church friend, Donna, from my original *Experiencing God* study group, was one of the servers for the weekend. I had told her weeks ago that God was working on me about something, but I wasn't ready to share any more information. I led her to where we could see the woman, and merely pointed to her. Donna looked at the woman in confusion, until her eyes settled on the front of the shirt. Her eyes got wide.

"So that's your secret? To adopt an orphan?" she asked in amazement.

I just shook my head and laughed. And cried. But for the first time, they were happy tears. I would have never seen the woman wearing my "billboard" if I had not been sitting on the aisle and opened my eyes at just the right time.

Everything for the rest of the weekend was mystical and God-filled. We watched a video about (what else?) an orphan boy begging for food, being rejected, and finally finding a place where many boys were playing games with two priests. I couldn't decide if it was a school or an orphanage, but they invited him to join them. Then he was happy. All the others were happy too.

During our weekend, we received cards and letters from friends, family, and previous Emmaus pilgrims. I treasure the letters of love and encouragement from my friends and family, but the ones from people who did not even know me inspired me. One such note included a little story:

> An old man and his grandson were walking along a deserted beach at sunset. The little boy became concerned about all the starfish that had washed up on the beach. He bent down, and one by one began to return them to the safety of the waves.

> "What do you think you are doing?" said the old man gently to his grandson.

> I'm throwing these starfish back into the ocean," said the little boy. "It is low tide now, and all of these starfish have been washed up onto the shore. If I don't throw them back into the sea, they'll die up here."

> "I understand," replied the old man. "But there must be thousands of starfish on this beach. You

can't possibly get to all of them. There are simply too many. And this is probably happening on hundreds of beaches all up and down this coast. Can't you see that you can't possibly make a difference?"

The little boy smiled, bent down and picked up yet another starfish. As he threw it back into the sea, he turned to his grandfather and said, "I made a difference to that one!"

The next day, one of the women gave a "Spirit Talk" about her journey of adoption. I was beginning to wonder if everyone here was considering adoption. No one knew of my secret agony and God's plans for me here in West Virginia, yet almost every aspect of my experience revealed God's activity.

I returned home fired up, convinced I could do this, and so full of God's spirit. But within a week I was asking God once more, "Please God, if you really want me to do this, give me a sign." I could imagine God throwing His hands in the air, giving up on me, because I was so unworthy of this assignment.

For months I ignored God. I was too busy to think about God or adopting. All fall I was, once again, caught up in preparing for the Maryland Christmas Show. This was my third year of participating, and I was starting to have repeat customers. This was my opportunity to earn college money. I sculpted and sewed every spare moment.

Christmas came and went, and I didn't feel that anyone was missing from around the tree. As a matter of fact, there was not room for another child around our Christmas tree, nor in my tightly closed heart.

Chapter Eleven

"He is there and He is not silent."

Francis A. Schaeffer

The phone call I had made to Frank Adoption Center in August to express an interest in the Russian children who visited with the Cherry Orchard Program had landed me on the agency's mailing list. That was safe enough; I was under no obligation. I knew it would be months before the Cherry Orchard Program delivered another group of hopeful children. I had some breathing room. I scarcely looked at the mailings from the adoption center until the early spring of 2001.

The "Calendar of Events" caught my attention. The last Thursday of every month, newly adoptive parents and those considering adoption met. I decided to go. Bruce was busy. A former guidance counselor from Linganore High School was there with her husband, her biological daughter, about five, and her newly adopted daughter, about two years old. The family attended to share their experience. It was quite a story. Her husband held the young fair-haired baby from Russia with such tenderness and affection. He genuinely loved this baby already.

They discussed the referral process, which was more complicated than I had thought. Choosing a sex and approximate age, and deciding what country and region where the adoptive parents would travel would be the first items to decide. I had no idea where to begin in that process. I had felt for months that God wanted us to adopt an older child, maybe from Russia, but I couldn't be sure. "Older child" when speaking in adoption language meant any child five years old and older. They were the most difficult to place because the majority of those adopting wanted infants, partly because of the risk of developmental delays that faced the older children.

And from what region? People had personal preferences. Some preferred China, or South America, or Russia, to name a few. I had felt God directing me to Russia; however, even if we could narrow it down to Russia, Russia was a huge country.

I could not "choose" a child—I wanted God to choose one for me, if, and this was still a big if, I adopted at all.

After adoptive parents determined desired ages of children and region, they were given a "referral," which was a file and video about one child or sibling group. One could have doctors look at the medical records and watch the video of the child to determine possible problems and treatment. If parents believed this child wasn't a proper fit, another referral would be given. But we could not take several referrals and choose our favorite child. We could look at only one child at a time. That made sense; I had no choice in what kind of child God gave me the old fashioned way!

The next family to share their experience that evening was the couple who had adopted the cute, smiley boy from last year's Cherry Orchard Program. The spunky personality that they described fit perfectly with my mental image of the boy. Their love, too, was real. I heard no regret or stories of ruined lives. But one part of their conversation particularly made me sit on the edge of my seat and listen, almost in disbelief. I suddenly felt like a captive member in an initiation of a secret society of "called adoptive mothers." First without my knowledge, and then against my will, I had been lured to this moment as my life's story was being unveiled. Again, there was that dreaded far away roar of peril ahead.

The new mother spoke of how she had a strong feeling that this is what they were supposed to do. They had married when they were both forty and had no desire or plans to have children. She casually read the invitation in the newspaper to host a Russian orphan for the Cherry Orchard Program, the one that I had so adamantly rejected! Suddenly she started seeing and hearing about Russian orphans wherever she turned. She couldn't shake the feeling that they were supposed to adopt. So, just like that, she persuaded her new husband to commit to, not only hosting little Dima, but to accepting him as their new son. They made it all sound so easy.

I marveled at her ability to change the direction of her life so abruptly, almost on an impulse.

I am not an impulsive person. I rarely buy anything on a whim. When I do, I usually head back to the store, receipt in hand, for a refund. I knew I could not return an adopted child!

It was about this same time I had a health scare. One morning during my shower, I noticed that a black discharge or blood oozed from one of my nipples when I put pressure on my breast. I gave it a couple of weeks to stop before I called for a doctor's appointment. My regular doctor saw me and referred me to a surgeon.

There, the nurse put me in an examining room and asked what the problem was. When I told her, she said with an awkward smile, "I'm going to put you in another room." I followed her down the hall to a smaller room. I undressed and waited on the table. This examining room's walls were filled with literature that was not on the walls of the previous room. There were posters about "what cancer cannot take away from me" and other inspirational messages about cancer and surviving it. The nurse must have thought there was a chance that I had cancer. Her unspoken concern made me uncomfortable, but the thought had already crossed my mind and entered my prayers.

When the doctor examined me, he said I would have to have

surgery to remove and biopsy a duct. He had a gentle and reassuring manner, but he did say that cancer could be the problem. But I was calm. All I could think of was that God would not give me the assignment to adopt, only to let me die before I could do it. I was certain that surgery would reveal that I was okay.

Back at my family practice, I had to go for pre-op tests, one being an EKG. It was a quick and painless procedure, administered by a nurse. Afterward, I was sent back to the waiting room until a doctor could look at the test. Soon a somber-faced doctor whom I had never seen before, introduced himself and asked if he could see me in his office. I followed him back and sat down. His serious manner scared me.

"Have you recently had a heart attack?" He began. The question took me by surprise.

"No," I answered.

"Well, you have either suffered a heart attack and were unaware of it, or you have some heart damage. I cannot sign off for surgery until you have seen a cardiologist," he warned.

I made the appointment with a cardiologist. I did have family members with a history of heart problems. Many of my relatives had died young because of heart disease. I still felt a calmness. God would not give me this assignment if I was not going to be able to carry it out. It occurred to me that the devil was putting roadblocks in front of me. He was trying to cause fear, and fear is always the enemy. Bruce was not willing to discuss the adoption option until we had all the medical tests and good news behind us.

I went through the stress test without any difficulty and returned the next day for the explanation of that test. As I sat waiting in my doctor's plush office, I heard his partner in the office beside me, praying with his patient. This was particularly reassuring to me.

"Thank you God," I said under my breath. He had led me through this with little fear.

When my doctor came in, he told me nothing that I didn't

already know: I had some irregularities in the rhythm of my heart, but it was normal for me. He didn't suspect any problems.

The next week I had breast surgery, which was as much a breeze as surgery can be. The worst of it was I was scheduled for 10 a.m., and they didn't take me in until 1 p.m. I was starving when I was abruptly awakened from anesthesia. I was instructed to eat lightly for a couple of hours. On the way home Bruce stopped a couple of blocks from the hospital at Burger King. I gulped my Whopper, and eyed Bruce's enviously as he guarded it suspiciously.

The next week, the verdict came in: I was fine.

I dragged Bruce along to the April meeting for Waiting Parents. One attractive woman, maybe in her late forties, talked of hearing about two brothers, again from Russia, who needed a home. She was a pediatrician, recently married. She was actually the pediatrician who looked over the referrals for the adoption agency. After seeing pictures of the boys, ages five and seven, she and her husband felt called to take them. She continued to say that they were Christians and had spent the week on their knees in prayer before deciding to take the boys. I felt ashamed that she spent a week deciding to be obedient, and I had been selfishly stomping my feet in defiance and turning away from God for over a year.

The other woman who spoke that night discussed her Russian-born daughter's attachment disorder and all the problems that they were encountering. The child bonded with everyone. They had difficulty helping her understand that *they* were her parents, and she couldn't go home with just anyone. Never once did I hear any regret—this was her child now. I was amazed at how seriously these adoptive parents took child-rearing. They researched it, attended workshops, saw counselors, and were intentional parents attempting to meet the challenges of their new children.

That night Bruce heard all the problems. I heard all the solutions. By some gentle leading by God, I was finally turning the corner. That did not mean though that I would not have to come around that same corner again and again, like a revolving door. But now I was at least staying in the vicinity of the door. Bruce would be a pushover when the time came. God would lead him too, like He did me, and our children. The adjustment to God's will had been the hard part for me, but it had changed me. God was real to me now, in a way that He never had been before. He had relentlessly pursued a relationship with me. No matter what happened in the future, whatever struggles our family would face, I would know that God was close; He was authentic; He was powerful. And He was *not* silent.

Bruce wouldn't be far behind in his revelation. He wasn't as selfish, or fearful as I. He didn't resist change as much as I did. He was always open to new adventures. This was certainly shaping up to be an adventure!

Chapter Twelve

"I gave in, and admitted that God was God."

C.S. Lewis

When the annual Youth for Christ Banquet came around again in April of 2001, Jacki and Steve Tate, who I hadn't seen since the previous year's banquet, invited me to ride with them. Bruce could not attend. I don't remember what triggered my sudden need to tell all, but in the car I started talking about the *Experiencing God* book, my *Walk to Emmaus* weekend, the "Faith is adopting an orphan" shirt, my cross falling off, my children's support, and my clear certainty about what God wanted us to do. There I sat, exposed by my confession. Their eyes were animated as they reacted with amazement at every detail. Many pieces of the puzzle were in place now. Knowing the evidence in favor of adoption was mounting, I continued to gush information, knowing all the time I should be silent, or these people of God might later wonder how I could refuse God's blatant invitation. Even if the Tates never mentioned it again, I would hold myself accountable because of their knowledge of the assignment.

For the entire half hour we rode together, I relived each experience. The hair on my arms spiked again and again, and I was aware of how astounding every piece of the puzzle was. I felt blessed to share this experience with them. I was amazed that the same God who had breathed the universe into existence, who lead Moses through the Red Sea and brought Jesus back to life, was up close and personal with *me*.

But the gentle cascades of hope that lured me toward the unknown waters of adoption alternated with the thrashing torrents of fear that threatened to crush me against sheer rock cliffs. The highs and lows of this journey, the true risks of commitment, and my own lack of faith contributed to my vacillating feelings about the voyage.

Weeks and months later when the Tate's would ask me where I was in the decision-making process, I was ashamed to admit that my resolve had faltered, and I was, once again, wavering. They would sympathize that it was truly a life-changing decision. They confided that they were glad God had not asked them to adopt an older Russian child, or any child, for that matter.

Again, for weeks I tread water against the ripping current, exhausted but determined not to venture closer to the danger that waited downstream.

More than a year had passed since the adoption theme had become a constant in my life. One morning at church we were reading the Prayer of Confession from the morning bulletin. I was alone, as everyone else in my family was attending a Sunday school function. Although I mechanically read the words without seeing them, I was suddenly aware of what I was reading. The prayer urged me to have a heart for the "poor and orphaned of the world." The quiet tears suddenly flowed. I made it through the service, but afterward, I sobbed uncontrollably.

A tragedy had shattered the Youth for Christ community that same week. Prayer requests were mentioned during the service, so my tears seemed appropriate. No one needed to know the real reason behind my near hysteria. After we returned home from church, I related the prayer for the poor and orphaned of the world to my family.

Kellie's face grew pale. "From what country did you say that you thought God wanted us to adopt?" She asked as though she held a secret piece of the puzzle.

"Russia," I answered as my anticipation for her secret welled up in me in the form of tears.

"We talked about Russian orphans in Sunday School today."

Taylor drew closer to the conversation, his eyes wide.

"We did too," he spoke slowly and played his own piece of the puzzle.

That was the day that I knew I could not continue to turn away from a waiting God. This was a battle that I could not win if I made God my opponent; even if I won, I would be the loser. I believed the logic of Jesus' preaching that to gain abundant life, one must be willing to sacrifice one's own life for God. Maybe I was being a bit dramatic. God wasn't asking for my life. He only wanted to modify my lifestyle. God was not asking me to sacrifice more than I could bear. I was beginning to realize my real sacrifice was to surrender control, to let God lead me down His path, to trust my fears to His care, to lay down this burden and not rush back to pick it up.

Once I started trusting a little, a peace came over me. I reminded myself, if God wants me to do this, it will bring glory to Him, and whatever ultimately happens, it will be positive. A watching world will see a loving God accomplish His perfect will.

A load was lifted when I realized that God would reveal Himself to many people through this adoption, and He would use our family! God's ways are always right. If people were going to see God at work, He wasn't going to show them my life in shambles! He would show something miraculous and awesome.

I had already seen glimpses of God's unrelenting love and power. He had worked in the lives of my family members to bring them on board with this mission He had assigned to all of us. The clues were so powerful and unmistakable. The puzzle was coming together so beautifully. God's presence was undeniable. He was in control of the radio and television, the newspaper, my subbing job, other adoptive parents, my money, my cross . . . God was in control. Period. And if I made myself available to Him, I could experience what God wanted for my family. If I could hang on to this assurance that I was doing what God had planned for my life and not backslide into selfishness . . . If I could do it . . . Why was there still such a big "if"?

The growing expectation of the powerful waterfalls ahead still struck a panicked chord in my heart. It was a reflex to flee, but back paddling against an impossible force only left me exhausted and helpless.

Chapter Thirteen

"Only he who believes is obedient and
only he who is obedient believes."

Dietrich Bonhoeffer

Just because I had reluctantly surrendered my will and resigned
myself to the fact that I had to adopt didn't mean I was always
happy about it. The dread of the annual Cherry Orchard visitation
program scheduled for August hung over me like a scheduled heart-
ectomy. What was wrong with me? Since I had become a reader of the
Bible, I had noticed a pattern in the Old Testament: when kingdoms
did what was right in the sight of the Lord, they flourished. Then the
next generation turned away from God. Their self-reliance usually
brought suffering. Then they would cry out to God; He would hear
their plea and save them; then they would do what was right in the
sight of the Lord. Over and over this cycle repeats itself in the Old
Testament. I was beginning to feel like a perfect illustration of how
that happens! As soon as I surrendered to the will of God, I had
peace and joy; however, almost in the same breathe, I was, once
again finding angles to escape God's plan.

When we went to Holden Beach in North Carolina in July, I
acknowledged beauty and pleasure in every moment. I walked the

beach, and I rode my bike up and down the eight-mile island trying to imprint the memory of this glorious life I had lived. I would look out over the vast blue-gray body of water, fixed on the horizon. Just out of sight over the skyline, the sea continued. There was so much more than I could see. The depth of the ocean seemed limitless; as much life lived hidden below the calm surface as above. I was a minuscule gear in the machinery of God's universe. Still, God wanted to involve me in His plan.

I tried to take mental snapshots of every event. I hugged my children sometimes longer than they wanted to be hugged. I wanted to freeze time. I did not want the week to end; I did not want to go home to the dark uncertainties of what lay ahead.

Shortly after we returned home, I got the dreaded call from Frank Adoption Center. I knew they would be calling about the Cherry Orchard program, but the call did not convey what I expected, what I was struggling to cheerfully anticipate. Sharon told me apologetically that the program had been cancelled for 2001. She shared no details, promising to contact me when she knew more.

"Cancelled!" I whispered in disbelief as I hung up the phone, wrestling with my guilt for feeling a bit relieved. But I had been so sure this was God's will for us. Now what?

The thought suddenly occurred to me this might be a test. I grabbed onto this possibility! Maybe God was testing me to see if I would go through with it. I had come pretty close. I was pretty confident I would have adopted a foreign orphan. But, of course, being sure was easy now, since it might never happen!

Maybe instead of adopting, I would help another couple who genuinely *wanted* to adopt by giving them money, as much money as I could raise. Maybe I would give a *lot* of money. We had college funds for the kids. I would be willing to give it all. I talked to my friends about this new plan and asked for prayers. My friend Jacki called one day to say she had found something that might be of interest to me. She knew I was searching for an easy out. She gave me a phone number she had heard on the radio, another message about those bothersome Russian orphans. I could call the number and donate money to send a child to a Christian Camp.

Perfect!

And yet, I never even called the number. Somehow that idea didn't settle me for long. The shirt had said "Faith is *Adopting* an Orphan," not sending one, or two, or all of them to a Christian camp! There was really no way out of it; adoption meant adoption.

Then my selfish, personal crisis over adoption moved to the back burner as 9/11 filled television screens, newspapers, and our personal lives with horror and sadness.

I was subbing in biology when Kris, one of my favorites (I had so many favorites by then!), ran into the silent class engaged in worksheets. "Can we turn on your TV? A plane just flew into the World Trade Center," he gasped.

I was trying to process this terrible accident while he was turning on the TV, not waiting for my reply. It was on all channels. Kris's hysteria riveted us all to the screen as we watched, in horror, as another jumbo jet seemed to disappear behind the other tower. An explosion of fire and debris horrifically appeared on the other side where we were expecting the plane to emerge. The room fell silent after the gasps in unison. We sat there, with our hands covering our mouths, blocking our silent screams, afraid to see, yet compelled to watch.

One boy turned to me and asked, so wanting a reassuring response, "What does this mean?"

I wished I had an answer. All I did know was it wasn't an accident.

That afternoon was surreal. All teachers were advised to turn off all televisions to circumvent further hysteria. Too late. The kids and teachers alike were starving for any information about the catastrophe. They did not want any cover-up. This was before everyone had cell phones, but there were televisions and radios throughout the school. The story continued to unfold and circulate: a plane crashed into the Pentagon, and another suspicious plane went down in rural Pennsylvania.

With our proximity to Washington, many of these students had relatives working at the Pentagon and other government agencies that might be targets of terrorism. I was only scheduled for the first two periods of the four-period school day. When I finished with my classes, I stayed and ran passes from the office to kids whose frantic mothers were arriving to take their children home. To safety? Where was "safe"? Our school and community were in the path from Camp David, about twenty-five miles to the northwest, to Washington, D.C., about thirty-five miles to the south, as the crow flies, or in this case, as the jet flies. Several times during the afternoon, ominous black fighter jets flew terrifyingly low, sweeping, circles over our school. The noise was deafening. Their interests were not in our school. They were concerned about our airspace!

In the midst of tragedy, patriotism filled Americans' hearts throughout the country. Linganore High School was no different. For a week and a half after the attacks, every morning the announcements were a vehicle for national pride. I wept as Lee Greenwood sang "I'm proud to be an American, where at least I know I'm free . . ." over the intercom system. The principal advised everyone to pray. In this public high school, we were abandoning senseless rules and asking for some serious help from a higher Power.

So much devastation. So much national pride. So many deaths and so many lives rearranged. Surely there must be orphans left behind—little Americans who spoke English, and hadn't spent their lives languishing in Eastern European orphanages, who probably were healthy, physically, and mentally, but needed new families.

I had a sudden hopeful thought. God had prepared me to adopt, but I might have mistaken the clues about *where* this child would come from. After all, the Cherry Orchard Program had been cancelled rather abruptly. There might be little Americans who needed me, right here in my own country. I enthusiastically surfed the internet, made calls, and could find no information about children who needed homes after so many parents were lost.

Sharon from the adoption center called me a few days later, with what she hoped would be welcome news in the midst of heart break: the Cherry Orchard visitation was back on, for October 18.

I was surprised the Russian Embassy would even allow the children to come to a country so recently under attack from terrorists. I expressed my concern about the safety of our country and for the children. Sharon reassured me that the terrorist attack would not prevent the children from traveling.

Okay, I was ready to relent. I was trying to get myself psyched up when Bruce reminded me that was the week of his annual camping trip with college and childhood buddies. He said he would cancel.

My hardworking husband looked forward to these trips. The phone calls and e-mails about them usually started in midsummer. He needed this trip every year to recharge his spirit. Maybe I could do the week by myself, with Heather's, Kellie's, and Taylor's help. I didn't have to ponder long, because Sharon called right back to say that the date had changed to November 5. Bruce would be in Florida on business until November 8. Well, for three days I could manage without him. He would still have three days to get to know the child. While we were still discussing options, Sharon called back to say that the date had changed one last time. Now the children would arrive on November 8. I told Bruce if God was willing to be so accommodating, we certainly could keep the boy for a week.

In a training session for potential host families, the staff at the Center explained that the children didn't know they were coming to be considered for adoption. I had been anxious that the children would get their hopes up and be disappointed. They must have seen other children being adopted from their orphanages. Surely they must have had some hope that maybe one day a new family would claim them. The staff reassured me that, even if we did not adopt, they could get to know these children during their visit and be better equipped to place them with other waiting families. All the children from last summer's Cherry Orchard Program had been adopted, and not all by the families who had hosted them.

The staff gave us other stark and real-life warnings about the problems that these children might experience. Of course there were the anxieties one would anticipate from children staying with strangers, compounded by the language difference. But other warnings included the possibilities that the children might not be toilet trained, or might wet the bed, or might not know how to use eating utensils. They were trying to be honest and informative, but they painted a challenging picture.

Even so, I called back with the go-ahead. There was fingerprinting and other paperwork that kept me occupied for most of October. At last I went to the adoption center to deliver the final forms. Sharon asked if I wanted to see pictures of the little boy we would be hosting. For some reason, I was surprised that they had pictures. I was suddenly afraid to see him. I held my breath as she opened his folder and handed me two black and white photocopies. The little boy who smiled back from the grainy photo surprised me. I don't know what I had expected, but this little Roman Igorevich Sudzhashvili was not it. The invisible child that I had agonized about for a year and a half had a vacant stare. He was a damaged child, that haunting child of my imagination. Beautiful little Roman's toothy grin was genuinely happy. This could have been a photo of any American child. With this face came a personality, a history, and a future. Then began the dreaded quivering of my chin that I knew from experience would lead to quiet tears and loss of speech. I swallowed hard and fought to respond.

A whispered, "He's beautiful," is all I could force out. Sharon understood. She must have seen other women whose emotions were right on the surface like mine in her experiences at the adoption center.

I gazed at the pictures a long time before I trusted myself to speak again.

"How long has he been in the orphanage?" I don't know what made me ask. Until the question popped out of my mouth, I had assumed he had lived there his whole life.

She picked up the typed pages and searched for the answer.

"Since . . . March of 2000," she read.

As I processed the answer, chills went down my arms. I remembered Anthony, the boy whose kindness on my first day of subbing inspired a note of thanks. I had written the note in March of 2000, when the unwelcome idea of "ADOPTION" first exploded across the screen of my mind.

"That's when I first started considering adopting," I responded excitedly. (Okay, so I exaggerated about my willingness from the beginning, over a year and a half ago.)

What she said next raised chill bumps on top of my chill bumps and reminded me of that secret society of "called adoptive moms."

"You've been listening," she whispered.

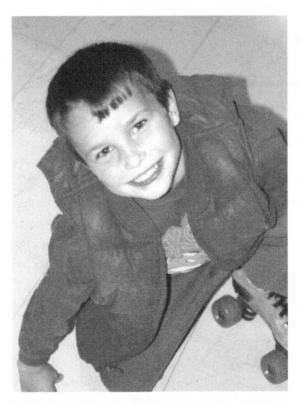

Roman Igorevich Sudzhashvili, age seven

His biography Sharon sent home with me was enlightening and disturbing. Roman had been removed from his family because of neglect, along with his eighteen-month-old brother, Rostislav, and his fifteen-year-old sister, Liana. Could I split up a family, or what was left of a family? Roman and his sister were found begging in the streets for food. The sister hadn't attended school in years. The mother and father, both parents of all three children, must have had some happiness in their marriage; it had lasted at least fifteen years. The report spoke of alcoholism and drug use by both parents. *Alcoholism and drug use.* I already knew there was a high likelihood of Fetal Alcohol Syndrome with many of these children. That possibility threatened to stir panic within me.

I wept as I read the translated documents. The mother accepted the charge of her drug and alcohol abuse, blaming much of it on her difficult financial situation; she vowed to improve her behavior and restore her parental rights. Roman was relinquished to Mozdok Home for Children, and Liana was enrolled in a trade school. Their mother had only ten days to make a dramatic change in her life and apply for reinstatement of parental rights. That resolution had expired two years ago. I could only imagine what that poor woman's life must be like now. The economy of Russia had created many such stories of broken families and destroyed lives.

I could not get Roman's baby brother and older sister out of my mind. I had heard warnings of people traveling to Russia expecting to adopt one child, only to discover the existence of multiple siblings. Without any time to consider all the ramifications, they had returned home with three or more children. That was before the new law that required two trips to Russia. Now, with the two trip rule, the cost of adopting went through the roof. If we met a brother or sister while there, were we prepared to return to Russia to rescue them too? I called Sharon and asked what the agency knew of the siblings. They had no information on either child. Because of his young and desirable age, the baby might have been adopted domestically, and not entered an orphanage where he could be traced. They suggested that the sister, now seventeen and a half, was probably considered unadoptable because of her age.

So the family was quite possibly already separated.

We braced ourselves for a November 8 invasion.

I scoured the house like we were expecting dignitaries! Bruce said I was "nesting." So I was. I was preparing my nest for another baby. I had done it with every pregnancy. Bruce kept reminding me that we were just *hosting* this child; he still needed time to consider a permanent commitment. I was aware that this situation must have made Bruce nervous. It was a thousand times more dangerous than bringing a lovable puppy home on approval. Any control over the situation that Bruce had seemed to have at one time must have appeared to be slipping away from him. He had been willing to investigate the possibilities of adopting, but suddenly we had a foreign child with a sketchy background coming to live with us for a week.

Bruce told his parents what we were considering, and they felt blindsided. Bruce had chosen not to tell them what he thought might be worrisome information until it was necessary. It was worrisome, and they wanted to talk about it before we ruined our lives. Two weeks before the boy was scheduled to visit, Bruce's parents, Mike and Betty, arrived with somber faces. They thought we were out of our minds, and they came to talk some sense into us. The discussion went badly.

Adopting an unknown, non-English-speaking older child who had endured who-knew-what was terrifying for my in-laws, who had been wonderful to us for twenty-four years. They had never interfered in our lives. When my friends complained about their in-laws, I could never relate, because mine had been so generous with their love, time, and support, as well as their resources. Hurting them was painful. They pointed out that we could help in a number of ways other than bringing a stranger into our home and subjecting our children to some vast wasteland of an unknown future. We could send money, they suggested. We could help poor and disadvantaged children in our own community. We had so much going for us, why would we risk, and possibly ruin, everything? It was difficult to argue with their position, points that I too continued to wrestle with.

But what about God's position?

I never said a word. Bruce did all the talking, and I sat there with a blank expression on my face, unable to contribute to the conversation. At one desperate point, they tried to appeal to my sound judgment. Evidently, they thought this was Bruce's insane scheme. He took the brunt of their hostility. Bruce never once gave me up by telling them this was my idea.

But it *wasn't* my idea. Yet, I did feel a little guilty sitting idly by without confessing that the inspiration had come to me and not their son.

We must have seemed unyielding, because the arguments became more and more desperate, with my father-in-law finally warning us that he would never step foot in our house again if we continued down this dismal path.

I didn't want to be like Job. I didn't want to sacrifice everything dear to me to be obedient to God. I remembered how disturbing it was to me reading how God had allowed Satan to bargain with Him over Job's soul. "Consider your servant Debbie" Satan was saying, and I wasn't looking much like a servant. God let Satan take away everything but Job's life to test his faith and faithfulness. I did not want to have my shallow faith tested. I had already failed too many tests involving my faith.

I was actually weighing whether the comforts of this life and my family, here and now, were worth ignoring the consequences for the rest of this life, and for the next. It was a profound but ridiculous comparison. Of course eternity should trump the comforts of the present, but yet I was tempted to surrender my allegiance to the known. The reality of that temptation and the certainty of its consequences terrified me and saddened me to my core. I was positive that disobedience in this life would mean consequences in the next. It was a torturous contemplation. There was no way out, at least no way that would please everyone.

I stubbornly clung to my comfortable lifestyle. I was afraid to commit to a child with needs I had no experience dealing with. My children were bright students and compliant children. What would I do with a child who struggled? Ominously, the word "delays" kept popping up at the meetings I attended, "delays" in some of the children's aptitudes. What if this child who God had in mind for me was never capable of living independently of Bruce and me?

"God!" I cried out, always thinking of myself, "Do I have to suffer devastation in order to be obedient?" I was prepared for little life adjustments, but not for life destruction.

"Please God," I begged, "If we must do this, please, just let him fit into our family. I know that I will not *love* him like the others, but please let the adjustment be tolerable for all of us."

How quickly I had forgotten the "problem" children at school who always found a way into my unsuspecting heart.

Chapter Fourteen

*"What saves a man is to take a
step—then another step."*

C. S. Lewis

The children arrived as expected on November 8, 2001. Kellie and I went to pick up our little stranger at 3:00 p.m. in the fellowship hall of a church in downtown Frederick. I was nervous during the half hour drive. I had worn make-up and fixed my hair. I wanted him to like us. I was shaking by the time we arrived in Frederick. I was glad to have Kellie along to attempt the impossible—to keep me calm.

We entered the fellowship hall in the basement of the church. The adoption center staff, Lisa, Martha, and Sharon watched me enter with animated grins and wide eyes.

"He's a wild one!" Lisa said, enunciating each syllable.

My heart plummeted! I did not want a wild one! "God, you didn't tell me this," I thought as I struggled with the prospect. I had little experience dealing with out-of-control children, except at school, and I didn't have to take them home with me!

I searched the faces of the children until I saw him. He looked up at us as he ate an apple, and his gaze held. He didn't glance away or show any other signs of being timid. He did look like a spirited boy! I fought back tears at seeing for the first time, at the age of seven, this wild boy who I knew immediately would become my son. Soon distracted by his little friend, he was off to play. I could not take my eyes from the small boy wearing jeans that swallowed him, a worn, brown sweater, and plastic boots I would later discover were two sizes too small. He was a beautiful child with shiny dark hair, hazel-green eyes fringed with thick lashes, and a creamy complexion. When he smiled, his whole face smiled. He had little dimples on the side of his face beside each eye. His little nose was splattered with freckles. He was positively adorable.

Refreshments were served, and we met the entire Russian entourage. The group of five children and four adults had arrived the evening before. Perhaps to prevent exhaustion and crankiness, they had spent the night in a hotel and rested most of the day, before the children were sent off with their respective host families. Little Roman hadn't seemed to have settled down from all the excitement. I learned that Dima, the official translator, had shared a sleepless night in the hotel room with Roman, and had first hand insight into this boy's electric personality!

The school superintendent, principal of the orphanage, the coordinator of the region, and the translator mingled and tried to answer questions about the children. Roman came to ask one of the bilingual women a question. When he had spoken in Russian, she turned to me and said, "He wants to know what color car you have."

Boys are the same no matter where they come from!

As Roman and his friend Yevgeniy waited in anticipation for the answer, I told her red. She translated for the boys. Their eyes grew wide, and there was back slapping and whooping. The word must have conjured up images of speed and wind whipping through seven-year-olds' hair. I knew this was the right answer—but the wrong car. I knew he was probably going to be disappointed to learn the color was wasted on a thirteen-year-old Ford Taurus station wagon.

Yevgeniy and Roma, 2002

As we left with our little charge, the Russian translator, Dima, encouraged me by saying through his thick Russian accent, "You are a brave woman." They all laughed, and another added, "You are our hero." I didn't panic. Roman was such a charming little guy, so healthy and vibrant. And I knew a lot of good parents whose children were prescribed Ritalin! God knew what He was doing.

Roman was a happy boy. That smile could not lie. Whatever had gone wrong in his life, clearly he had also experienced joy, trust, and love. He was full of life and energy, until we got in the car, then he was utterly silent. This boy who had so much to say to his fellow countrymen knew it would be to no avail now, on Kellie and me. When we stopped the car and got out, the spark visibly drained from his small, wiry body. He leaned against the wall of the garage, where he remained for the next hour and a half, and cried.

Taylor came and tried to distract him. Two neighborhood families came down to meet him. They played ball outside the garage, trying to entice him, but still the tears ran down his dirty little face, leaving muddy smudges. He would periodically stop crying and watch with keen interest until someone would try to urge him out. Then he would cry again. It was going to be dark before long, and I was getting desperate. I called the adoption center, though I knew the staff would be entertaining the delegates. I made calls to several locations, until finally I was able to leave a message. Within twenty minutes Martha, the social worker, called, and after hearing my dilemma, put Dima on the phone to talk to Roman. Roman talked in quick Russian for less than a minute, put the phone down on the hood of the car and then answered the coaxing of my neighbor to come out and play ball.

He was all smiles, and it was as if he had never been sad. He kicked the ball and displayed his soccer prowess, ordering the older boys to locations, and they were quick to respond. I don't know what Dima had told Roman, but it was visibly comforting and reassuring to the young boy. Maybe he explained that they would all be together again tomorrow. I imagined what it must be like for a seven-year-old to be half way around the world from home, staying with complete strangers, and those strangers could not even understand plain Russian!

It was unseasonably warm that week of November, so the children played outside until long after dark. When they came inside, the child sat down on the floor and with some effort, pulled off the plastic boots that he had slid all over the driveway in. He never cried when he fell and skinned his hand. He grimaced as he uncurled his toes that had been turned under in order to fit into the boots. Each little toe knuckle was callused from the too-tight boots. He rubbed the sore toes a minute and was soon off to investigate the house. I bought him new Nike sneakers the next morning.

He was a terrible eater. I was surprised; I had been told these children would probably be hungry and would eat anything. He didn't want any meat—we had prepared steak. He took one bite of the bread and didn't like that either. He was ecstatic to find potatoes in the refrigerator while he was investigating. I microwaved him one and, although I urged him to wait until it cooled, he peeled it, juggling it from hand to hand. He was decidedly assertive, not at all what I was expecting.

We kept calling him "Roman." He firmly and politely corrected our pronunciation. He held up his little hand with long fingers, palm toward us as if to say "wait."

"Roman, nyet." (We learned "nyet" meant "no" before he came. I thought that might be one word we would need.) He spoke slowly and intentionally, because we were, after all, mere Americans. "Roma." He spoke slowly and deliberately, rolling his "R" in a way I knew my Southern version would never match. My flat "Roma" would never sound as musical as his.

"Rrrroma," we all practiced until he was satisfied with our efforts. I wondered how we moved from being the adults to being his eager-to-please pupils! I sensed a foreshadowing of things to come!

For his much-needed bath, he locked himself in the bathroom, leaned over the bathtub, and got the top of his head wet. I knocked on the door about this time. He opened in the middle of getting dressed in his new pajamas I had purchased for him. When I saw his muddy little smiling face, I smiled sternly at him and pointed back to the tub. He laughed and pointed to his almost wet hair, hoping I would be mindlessly convinced that he had bathed. I picked up the dry bar of soap, and he laughed, knowing he was busted. He got back in the tub, in his underwear and he let me shampoo his hair and bath him.

When bedtime came, he was adamant that he was not going to bed. I just sat at the head of the bed and started to read a colorful children's book aloud. He was curious enough to want to see the book, and was soon lying beside me. He studied the pictures carefully and, although he could understand no words from the English book, sat attentively for ten minutes. I was encouraged. Maybe the diagnosis of hyperactivity the staff had freely identified for me earlier that afternoon was premature.

He wanted to sleep with the door closed and no night light. He fell asleep immediately. I, however, did not. I was afraid he might wake, come out of his room, and fall down the stairs right outside his door. I left the bathroom light on down the hall.

I slept fitfully, my dreams were haunting. I dreamt this was not the boy God wanted me to have. Everything had gotten mixed up. He wanted me to adopt Yevgeniy, Roma's friend. Yevgeniy had severe scoliosis, as was, from what I had observed in our brief meeting, a quiet little gentleman, the polar opposite of his live-wire friend! Though he was ten, he was no taller than Roma, and Roma was small for his age. Yevgeniy would be examined later in the week by an orthopedic surgeon who would report that his spine could be corrected by one surgery. Did God intend for him to be my boy? His host family was not intending to adopt him. They had adopted the previous year from Kazakhstan. They were hosting him so he could come to the United States to be medically evaluated. Information could be gathered about him for other prospective families. The dreams would continue to haunt me when I was awake. I worried everything had been confused. Now how would I know God's will? Should I proceed?

Roma would forget sometimes that we couldn't speak or understand Russian, and rattle off questions. I could tell they were questions by the intonation of his husky little voice and the earnestness on his face. I would, of course, not know how to respond, so I would simply say, smiling, "Blah, blah, blah." He was extremely amused by that surprising response and answered, "Blah, blah, blah." He had a delightful sense of humor. Sometimes when he would talk, I would just answer, "Yeah, yeah, whatever." This would amuse my own children, and cause Roma to laugh as well, though he had no idea what we were, or he was, laughing at. He soon felt comfortable with us. Laughter is indeed a universal language.

Verbal communication turned out to be a non-issue. He had no trouble making his wishes known to us. And I quickly became proficient with the word "no" in Russian.

"Nyet!" I said often in close pursuit of the energetic little guy. I resigned myself to the possibility a professional might still need to make a diagnosis about possible hyperactivity. Roma was exhausting! My friends who saw him in action assured me he was simply "all boy." Taylor was always quiet, either reading or constructing miniature cities with Lego and Knex building blocks. I was unprepared for Roma's busyness.

One day we were invited to take Roma to Jacki and Steve's farm. They were eager to meet Roma. These were our "Youth for Christ" friends who had become fascinated with the story I had related to them six months earlier. They had been extremely supportive, first by suggesting a way out when it was apparent that was what I was so desperately searching for, by suggesting sending money to a Christian camp for Russian orphans. Then later, as they heard the undeniable stories of God's involvement and finally the conviction in my voice, they gently encouraged us to take the first tiny steps.

At the farm, Roma was allowed to feed the horses from his hand and to drive the giant green tractor while sitting on Steve's lap. Of course, then he wanted to drive our car home, too! The next day a neighbor brought down his Harley Davidson to take Roma for a ride. Other neighbors brought down abandoned toys from their older children. Everyone was captivated by this tiny, smiley boy.

His favorite toy was a car console with a steering wheel with buttons and levers. He was a fast and dangerous driver; I could tell by the sound effects he made: screeching tires and crashing! One button, when pushed, sounded a recording of a child's voice saying, "Are we there yet?" Soon Roma, in perfect English was walking through the house repeating, "Are we there yet?" with no idea what he was saying.

Once a day, a planned activity with the rest of the Cherry Orchard kids and host families required our attendance. Roma was very affectionate at the daily reunions, high-fiving his friends, and hugging the adults. This assertive little boy intrigued me. I was impressed with his charm, openness, and confidence. I was encouraged by his intellect. After a few days of posing for his picture, and pose he did, he finished our count down for the camera. I don't know why we counted; he couldn't understand English! But he was learning! With the camera leveled at him, we would say slowly "one, two…," Roma added "Free." "One, two, free."

Taylor had been ready to step into the influential role of a big brother, but Roma was experiencing stimulation overload. He didn't behave as Taylor had expected. Taylor had expected a timid, quiet boy, who would follow him around devotedly. Instead, Taylor thought Roma was a brat. Taylor confessed he didn't know it was going to be this hard. There was reality. There was jealousy. My heart was breaking for my baby. I had seen too many kids at school punish their parents by practicing destructive behavior, not realizing they often suffered more than the parent. I did not want Taylor to experience feelings of neglect and then react in ways that might harm him. In his young summation, he might think we loved Roma more. A Pandora's Box of disastrous possibilities flooded my mind. I could not do this if it would hurt Taylor in any way.

One of our daily activities with the group was a Thanksgiving theme dinner at a mountain lodge. The children played happily while the host families enjoyed the pot luck dinner and fellowship. Some families from previous Cherry Orchard programs had been invited. It was a beautiful day in the Catoctin Mountains, but it was a gloomy day in my heart. Roma seemed so happy when reunited with his fellow Russians. Why would we take him out of his comfortable existence and force upon him what we believed was best for him? Were Americans justified in taking these children away from their homeland, their culture, their simple way of life, even if these lives seemed impoverished by our standards? How could we assume our decadent lifestyles were better and more valuable than these children's heritage? Bruce and I talked to Dima. Dima had grown up in Russia. He would know the truth.

He paused a long time before he answered.

"Roma is a happy boy. His life is not so bad *now*. But as he grows . . ." Dima searched for words to help us understand. His eyes grew dark as he continued, "There are estimates as high as four million orphans and homeless children in Russia. Most of them live on the streets or in the underground sewers. Only the luckiest children live in orphanages, which are by no means ideal. Many facilities don't have hot running water or basic necessities. Many children run away from the orphanages, or are put out at the age of sixteen, or younger. Of those kids, fifty percent are high risk, forty percent abuse drugs and alcohol, forty percent resort to crime, and ten percent commit suicide. Many young girls are forced into prostitution. The life expectancy is lower than average for these kids. There are few opportunities. Only ten percent become a functioning member of society."

He painted a dismal picture for us.

My future seemed dismal too. It was almost an effort to continue breathing. I could not even look at my Taylor, who had made the effort to join us, but did not know what to do with himself now that he was here. Roma ignored him now that he was with his friends. Taylor's pain-filled face told me his vote. But did he have a vote anymore?

One day I escaped to sub, and Bruce took off the day to go roller skating with the group. I was paralyzed all day by fear.

If God knew everything, and He thought I could do this, why couldn't I just do it? Bruce came home with the same sentiment: he couldn't do it either. We were both feeling terribly old and extremely tired.

On the last night Roma was with us, Bruce went to talk to his parents, again. They lived about an hour away. Roma wouldn't be awake much longer, but Bruce felt he needed to see his mother and father. When he left, he hugged Roma and told him that he loved him as I cried. Would Bruce ever see this little boy again? A fog of sadness settled in our house. Kellie, Taylor, and I all felt blue. Finally Taylor announced, "Well, I'm taking Roma downstairs to play."

"Play what?" I asked.

"We are going to fight."

I ran for my video camera.

Bruce and Taylor always "fought." I hated it. They were rough, and often Tay got hurt and cried, but the next night when Bruce came home, Taylor would beg for more, and I would resume fussing. Every night they would indulge in this barbaric recreation. One day Bruce brought an article home for me to read. It was about the roughhousing I complained about daily. This was how men bond, the article explained. From what I had witnessed, the author was right.

Tay was now willing to bond with Roma. My heart soared at the thought of it.

The two boys rolled over and off my new rec room sofa and chair. I didn't even wince. They laughed; they were rough; they were gentle. Once when Roma thought he had hurt Taylor, he put his little hand on Tay's shoulder and questioned with a concerned face to make sure everything was okay. When they finished "fighting," and I was never sure exactly how the end came to this game, something had changed.

Taylor, 2001, age 12

Roma and Tay then went upstairs to play with Legos. I called Kellie to come, and the three of us, sitting on the floor, held hands around Roma and prayed. We prayed for Roma's safe trip home, for Grandmommy and Granddaddy's peace about whatever we decided to do. We prayed we could know and do God's will. I don't even remember what all we prayed for, but Roma was uncommonly quiet and solemn while we prayed, aware something profound was taking place. At bedtime, he was reluctant to give up the fun and the attention. He didn't want to go to bed. God provided a perfect diversion: our friend Jacki called with car trouble and needed to be picked up. Taylor chose to stay home. Kellie, Roma, and I were off to the rescue. They bundled up in the back seat, cuddling, and Kellie had her turn to bond, the way girls bond with small children. When we got home, he was ready to go to bed. I was still confused about adopting, but feared I would miss out on a special blessing God had intended for our family if I refused. Roma was certainly a lovable child. Someone somewhere would adopt him, if not us.

The next morning I readied Roma for his return to Russia. He proudly wore his new Nike sneakers, his Scooby-Doo watch, a Pokémon shirt, sweat pants, a red down vest, and a Baltimore Orioles baseball cap. He looked thoroughly American. His worn, brown sweater, plastic boots, and enormous jeans were crammed in the bottom of a backpack leftover from my kids. His miniature green John Deere tractor, a gift from Steve after the tractor ride, new clothes I had bought him, and a small album of photos of our family and his trip were on top for easy access. We met the others at 7:30 a.m. at an elementary school for a short music program. Afterwards, the visiting children from Russia and the American school students would plant a cherry tree, the week's closing activity symbolizing world friendship. The Russian delegates, one a principal from the orphanage, got a tour of the relatively new school. During the tour, Roma was always up front with the school's principal, leading the way.

Martha said, "I have a feeling wherever Roma goes to school, he will know the principal."

I laughed, knowing this was true, but not necessarily the way she meant it. Martha had been present to witness his initial busyness. She collaborated in the preliminary "wild one" diagnosis the adoption agency staff and Russian ambassadors had delivered to me with such amusement. They only had a hint at what I had discovered about this boy during the past week: he was a curious, intelligent, kind, well-mannered, and energetic boy who thrived on being where the action was. Roma was a leader. If he had questions, he would ask; if he had ideas, he would share. His little swagger spoke volumes of his self confidence; his quick warm smile spoke to me of his capacity to love and to trust. This little child of God, could he be my child?

Was I even worthy to be his mom?

The kids all piled into the van to go to the airport. Roma was the first one in, escaping my hug, and waved happily from the very back seat. While one host mom wept while hugging her two young wards she had no intention of ever seeing again, I shed no tears. I walked to my car and rode home, numb.

What next?

That night our house was gravely quiet. I was too tired to think, but my children asked the question I was not ready to answer. Kellie was in love with the little boy who put his head in her lap and held her hand.

"Mom, we have to adopt him," she pleaded.

Taylor was more subtle, in keeping with his nature. He put on is therapist hat again, "You know, Mom? I don't think God is doing this for Roma." He paused and I could see him think. His chilling declaration reminded me that the decisions we made at this instant would affect the rest of our lives.

He took a deep breath and ventured out a little further, leading me out into swift currents that pushed us downstream at an alarming rate.

He spoke cautiously, "Our lives will change forever, no matter what we do. If we adopt him, our lives will definitely change." We both smiled, knowing this was very true. "And if we don't, our lives will never be the same because we will always wonder about him."

I was afraid he was right, but I wanted neither of those options, especially if Taylor was in jeopardy!

He took one more critical step out, watching me, hoping he would not regret his next words for the rest of his life. "I think we should adopt him," he added.

I thought so too.

Chapter Fifteen

"If you try to save your life, you will lose it. But if you give it up for me, you will surely find it."

Matthew 11:28 (CEV)

Within a week, I would begin the arduous task of filling out the avalanche of paperwork that would culminate in my becoming the mother of another child, with all the risks and responsibilities. And all the rewards. But Bruce needed more time.

"I am almost forty-eight years old," he argued.

"God knows that" was my simple reply to every argument he offered, from "we will have two kids in college next year; we'll never be able to afford it" to "we only have four bedrooms." I flashed back to the tiny four room apartment of my childhood, where, for twelve years, my mother and three children happily carried on the business of a simple but happy life.

Bruce's parents were unyielding in their opposition. Poor Bruce was stuck in the middle of two extremely determined forces. I was sure the devil was behind my father-in-law's obstinacy, but he was equally certain the devil was fueling this fanatical decision he believed would devastate his family.

Although the senior Michaels had declined our annual invitation to come for Thanksgiving, we all piled in the car to visit them for the day, invited or not. Mike could hardly look at us, his disappointment and distain was apparent. Betty confessed that it would be easier if we lived 500 miles away, so they wouldn't have to see us again. She was in the middle of an imploding family, helpless to defuse the bomb. She was afraid for Bruce's ninety-six-year-old grandmother, Gigi, who was worried sick about the whole family. Betty said it would be on our conscience if something happened to Gigi. And Mike, whose health had been tenuous for years, suddenly had dangerously high blood pressure.

I didn't feel like it should be on our conscience if something happened to Gigi or Mike. We weren't getting a divorce, or going to jail, or doing anything that should cause such family shame. Our kids had been on board for a year and a half, and kids are by nature the most self-centered group in all of civilization. If *they* agreed to this mission, why should we care if anyone else objected? I wanted to scream at the injustice, but somehow I had the strength to smile at Mike, Gigi, and Betty, ignore the hostility, and tell them we loved them when we left.

My birthday was a few days later. Heather gave me the best gift of all: She made me a card. They always made cards that were such treasures to me. But this one was balm to a wounded heart. She wrote that I was truly her hero, that she was impressed that I was able to keep my composure when people around me were so unreasonably angry and negative. I didn't think she, or any of the kids had noticed. She had no idea I could not have kept from screaming if God had not had one hand on my shoulder, and the other over my mouth!

At Christmas, I was proudly passing around the photo album I had filled after Roma's visit, telling family and friends we were adopting: Bruce would nervously add "Maybe." Six weeks had passed since the children had returned to Russia. The adoption center called us with our options: begin the application process, or relinquish our first right to adopting Roma. If we rejected him, they would release his file to other prospective parents. His picture was on the bulletin board at Frank Adoption Center, along with all the other kids from November's Cherry Orchard Program. In one photo, Roma had his hands spread wide in the air, a big banner of a smile across his impish face as if to say, "Here I am world." He was a charmer. Could I ever forgive myself if I declined God's gift of Roma? I knew he would garner enthusiasm from other families who would be attracted to his exuberant smile and charisma. I was uneasy knowing that other families came into Frank Adoption Center daily and could fall in love with my son while Bruce was "thinking about it."

I was more determined than ever to be obedient to God. I remembered back to Henry Blackaby's book: "I have to get my heart into such a state that it has no will of its own." I had moments of that now. One day after a particularly brutal phone encounter with the Michaels, I was reading my Bible in Matthew 10:34–39 (CEV). "Not Peace, but Trouble" was the heading that caught my eye.

> "Don't think that I came to bring peace to the earth! I came to bring trouble, not peace. I came to turn sons against their fathers, daughters against their mothers, and daughters-in-law against their mothers-in-law. Your worst enemies will be in your own family.
>
> If you love your father or mother or even your sons and daughters more than me, you are not fit to be my disciples. And unless you are willing to take up your cross and come with me, you are not fit to be my disciples. If you try to save your life, you will lose it. But if you give it up for me, you will surely find it."

I dug my heels in, again.

Bruce confided that he was worried about what this could do to our family, and to our marriage. I was worried too, but the only thing I was sure of was that I had to do it, no matter what the cost.

I talked to a friend about Bruce's reluctance and my determination to move ahead with the adoption. I told her that I had to, with or without Bruce. After I had told her all of my arguments, she said the words I needed to hear.

"Debbie, God doesn't want you and Bruce to separate over this. This little boy needs Bruce too. What I am hearing from you is 'me, me, me.' I think you have to turn this over to God."

I recognized the wisdom in her inspired words and felt some relief.

The next morning as I prepared for church, I was experiencing one of those rare Sundays when I wasn't herding everyone out the door five minutes before the service started while still ten minutes from the church. I turned on TV where a preacher was in mid-sermon, but the part I heard was the essential part. "Sometimes we make it all about us. It's me, me, me." I sat frozen on the edge of the sofa. I didn't hear any more of his words. My friend's words were confirmed.

"Thank you, God." I said aloud. I knew Bruce and I would be okay.

We asked our Sunday school class to pray for my in-laws Mike, Betty and Gigi, and for every aspect surrounding this process. Our class had been an inspiration. This class had been a family to us. We had laughed and cried and worked and played together. These were godly, prayerful people, full of love and support. I asked my mother's prayer group in North Carolina to pray. My mother had always thought the adoption was a wonderful idea. Her faith in me in anything I did always gave me encouragement. Her faith in this project gave me faith that it was, without a doubt, God's will. My mother knows God.

My father-in-law was becoming belligerent, and I feared would never recant, having said, almost as a vow, things he would never again do with us. He said he would hire a lawyer and take Taylor away from us, since we were not fit to raise him. I was certainly able to understand my in-laws' fear. But they had not met this lovable boy. And they had not had to deal with God shaking them out of bed in the middle of the night and the never-ceasing barrage of adoption messages! Nor had they experienced God's incredible presence and His relentless love and affirmation in every little step I took toward obedience.

In this tug of war between God and my in-laws, I was being torn in two, but I had no question who was the strongest.

Chapter Sixteen

"Assuredly, I say to you, inasmuch as
you did it to one of the least of these
My brethren, you did it to Me."

Matthew 25:40 (NKJV)

Even though Bruce was still "thinking about it," I picked up the adoption application from the Frederick office of Frank Adoption Center. I could begin the procedure, just to get a head start while he was considering it. I was nervous about Roma's alluring picture hanging in their office. I wanted to appease the adoption center staff so they would tell other eager families to forget about my little boy. I imagined that many hopeful moms had fallen in love with Roma and that there was a long list of people who were hoping against hope that we would take a rain check on adopting, or be denied an opportunity to adopt on a technicality.

Bruce knew this ship of adoption was leaving the harbor, with or without him. He could hardly stand on the dock and hold the rope. He never officially granted me permission to move forward with the application, or to write the first $200 check that was required at the time of application. He had heard my stories, told and retold. He had known that adopting was not my idea—it was something I could not refuse or ignore. I did not fabricate stories to supply a means to an end. Bruce was a virtuous man, a wonderful, unselfish father, a submissive servant of God, and an awesome husband. I had prayed that God would share with Bruce what He had revealed to me, but no such revelation was forthcoming. Bruce would have to trust me. He had to come on board, or be left in the wake.

The trail of paperwork stretched ahead of me like the Great Wall of China. I hate paperwork. My mind doesn't do paperwork. I am certain that if labels of learning disabilities had existed when I was in school, I would have been branded with one. Or perhaps during the pity-parties of "I hate paperwork," I was just seeking an excuse to ask Bruce to fill out this formidable stack of official documents. I was a slow reader of this type of tedious text. Knowing the importance of following all directions and answering all questions, I scrutinized the dense package with an overwhelmed mind. I did not want to complete all this paperwork. I wanted Bruce to do it. But I knew Bruce was not going to do it; he was still hoping it might not even be necessary. So I set forth to knock out a few pages every day; even so, I would often misspell a word at the end of a page, answer on the wrong line.

Then the information about the fees intruded again. I knew it was expensive, but I didn't realize that the first figures I had received from the adoption center did not include traveling to Russia, and not traveling to Russia was not an option. Our plane fares to Moscow and to Roma's region, return flights back to Moscow and home for three of us, hotel and host family stays for nine days, the interpreter, coordinator, food, and land transportation added another five to six thousand dollars! Our total now was at $22,000. Twenty two thousand dollars! It was a lot of money. I struggled again with sticker shock as my conscience reminded me that one cannot put a price tag on the life of a child. But the next year we would have two kids in college. Kellie was considering Carnegie Mellon in Pittsburgh, and Heather was in her third year at Maryland Institute College of Art in Baltimore. We had saved for college. Did God want me to use that money? There were always loans. Most people got loans. But Bruce hated being in debt. We drove old cars so we wouldn't have a car payment. Our first mortgage was for ten years instead of thirty. Bruce hated being in debt. He also hated spending money.

I remembered the $100 I gave to a friend at the prodding of God, and the unexpected reimbursement. God had led me here. He must have a plan.

He did.

One day my neighbor and painting partner, Judy, called me. I say "painting partner" because we had recently painted murals on the walls of two homes. A year and a half earlier, she had asked if I were interested in painting wall murals with her. She knew I had a degree in art. She did not know I had not painted anything in years. I didn't feel confident enough to paint murals on walls, especially someone else's walls. I told her that I would think about it. Six months later she mentioned it again, and I impulsively said I would do it. We had two jobs right away, and then nothing for months. We wanted more work, but hustling jobs was not our forte. We had naively hoped that painting a few rooms in posh neighborhoods would spark the sin of covetousness, and create more jobs than we could handle. It was not to be. Our last job had been seven months earlier.

Judy said we might have an extensive job for a restaurateur her daughter had met at a golf tournament for his entire restaurant. It sounded like a long shot, and a restaurant was a bigger project than I thought we were even ready for. We struggled to work up a price, not really having any idea what we were doing. Then Judy went to meet with the owner one day while I was subbing at the high school. She returned and left a message on my answering machine. We had a job! Before she even told him what our price quote was, the aggressive man refused to hear our estimate. He offered us $10,000 to do the whole restaurant, take it or leave it.

Well, for professionals, $10,000 to paint one small and one large mural, fifteen marble columns, grapes and wine bottles and Italian city names might not be much money, but to us "pre-professionals," it was a fortune. Five thousand apiece! Materials would cost us about sixty dollars. We began right away. It took us eleven eight-hour days. The owner, employees, and patrons were delighted with the end results. We were thrilled with the finished murals, and the money.

Driving home our final afternoon, Judy remarked that she didn't know how we ever got that job.

I knew how.

Five thousand dollars and counting.

Steve and Jacki had expressed a commitment to helping us financially. I was thankful for their prayers, because they were on a first name basis with God. But the subject of money was awkward. In January we met them for dinner. They were always eager to hear my stories of God's work throughout this process. They said they were extremely inspired by what we were doing, and wanted to help. They pledged to give us $5,000 to offset our costs. Their gift far exceeded my expectations. I was truly touched as unexpected tears stung my eyes. I could not speak. My pride and sense of reason wanted to say, "we can't let you do that." Bruce was strangely silent too.

Sensing our uneasiness and anticipating our response, Steve continued. "We have prayed about this, and we truly feel that God is leading us to do it."

Jacki added, "And we are glad God is telling us to give money, and *not* adopt an orphan!"

They eased my discomfort and my uncertainty by their genuine and sincere response. Five thousand dollars was a gift beyond my comprehension. We thanked our friends across the table right after I thanked God. We had $10,000!

Frank Adoption Center had applied for a grant on our behalf. "A Child Waits" Foundation grants aid to families who adopt "special needs" children. Roma would qualify because of his age. Any child over five years old is considered hard to place. Everyone wants younger children. At one of our home studies in February, Martha casually announced, "Did Lisa tell you that you received the grant for $5,000?" God is good, all the time. We had $15,000 in our growing "Roma" account!

Our next installment came at tax time. We did our returns early, because Heather's scholarships required completion of the Free Application for Student Aid applications, or FAFSA. In addition, we usually got a refund which we were always eager to receive as soon as possible. When Bruce finished our tax forms, we were astounded to learn that we were due a reimbursement of $4,600, more than we had ever gotten back before, about double what we were expecting. One might argue that we had paid that in, that it really wasn't God's doing. To that, I would answer that $19,600 was earmarked for nothing but Roma!

I felt we could handle the remaining $2,000. There was one more grant that we found out about late. We almost missed the deadline. It was a state grant for $2,000 dollars. Bruce was skeptical. He worked for the state of Maryland. He knew the state budget had suffered like everything else in this post 9/11 economy. But we filled out the paperwork and mailed it in. We would have to wait sixty days to learn the outcome of that application.

Among the many documents and tests required by law for international adoption were multiple birth certificates for the entire family, marriage certificates, proof of pet vaccinations, water tests, a fire inspection, and AIDS tests for all family members over the age of eighteen living in the home. I wondered how we managed to bring the other children home from the hospital as babies without all of these credentials. Also, all members of the household had to have medical examinations. I had been unhappy for years with our family practice, with the doctor who had apathetically and incorrectly told me that I had suffered a heart attack. We had never changed, though I had threatened to do so many times. With physical exams required of all of us, I checked into other doctors in our insurance network.

There was a pair of doctors on the list who had once been part of the rather large practice we had been using, but who had opened an office together. It was a male doctor and a female doctor. Bruce and I had both seen them once for a checkup. I called my insurance company and had the whole family switched to their combined practice.

Then I went for my check up with adoption forms in hand. I was impressed with my doctor's warmth. She wasn't in a hurry. She examined me, pronounced I was in excellent health, and then asked me what had prompted the adoption. She seemed to be particularly curious.

Explaining the series of events behind my adoption experience was hard for me to share with people I didn't know, hard even with some that I did know. I squirmed and warned that it was a long story. I felt I should explain more. Finally I confessed, "I am a Christian, and I feel this is what God is calling me to do."

Her next question made the hair on my neck and down my arms stand up, like it did so often now. "You did know that I adopted two boys from Russia?"

Quick tears stung my eyes. I sat on the edge of the table and said that long "Noooo" that begs for further explanation.

"It really is a "calling," isn't it?" she said, revealing that she too was a member of the secret society of "called adoptive moms."

She understood. While other patients undoubtedly sat fidgeting impatiently in the waiting room, she related her similar story.

God had again confirmed that this was to be my calling. The doctor's experience, as all the other circumstances that converged to bring Roma to us and us to Roma, led me right back to the certainty that God had planned this all along.

But now instead of being mortified by the prospect, I was intrigued with my new relationship with God. This wasn't really my gig at all: God was the captain of this ship. All I had to do was trust and obey and be a kind of "first mate," albeit unqualified. I don't know why God wanted us to adopt a child from Russia, this

Roman Igorevich Sudzhashvili in particular, but He clearly wanted it. I was only capable of taking tiny steps, but that's all I needed to do. God continued to show me the way. He had proven to me beyond any doubt that He was always there, shining light on my path, encouraging me, loving me. What a relief to finally get it.

Chapter Seventeen

"The lord is my shepherd; I shall not want.
He maketh me to lie down in green pastures:
he leadeth me beside the still waters."

Psalm 23:1-2 (KJV)

In February Bruce went to Fairfax again to talk to his dad. He wanted to tell him in person that we were moving forward with our plans to adopt. I prayed nonstop while he was gone. All of our church friends were praying for a peaceful and loving resolution. I knew what being ostracized from his family would do to Bruce. Could our marriage survive that rejection? I wasn't sure.

When Bruce came in the door, I tried to read his expression. Bruce prides himself on surprising me. He said nothing at first; he just held me.

"They will never set foot in our house again," he began with no expression in his voice.

"Really?" I asked as I held my breath, not knowing whether to trust him.

"No," he smiled with tired relief, "they said it was our decision. They love us too much to let anything come between us."

I slumped in relief. This was exactly the reaction I had prayed for. I had not expected exuberance; I felt sure that would come later, when they got to know Roma and when they realized that our lives were not ruined by a careless impulse, but enriched by God's unexpected gift. I just wanted them to trust us and support our much considered decision, but mostly I wanted their love and support.

Bruce's elation was evident, and he was finally ready to move forward enthusiastically. He was a saint. I told him many times that had the situation been reversed, had it been he who had come to me and said God wanted us to adopt an orphan, I would have said that God had not spoken to me about it. I am sure I would not have been as trusting and accommodating as Bruce! God had spoken to me and still I had not been cooperative!

God knew that I would be the hard sell. He knew it would take me this long to relent, that He needed this time to prepare me to be a competent and eager mother to this boy whose own mother had been too troubled to mother him. His timing was perfect. This boy who entered the Mozdok Home for Children in March of 2000, after being removed from his addict parents for neglect, would be available for adoption when God got me ready. God can pull some strings. I later learned something even the adoption agency had not known when the children came for the Cherry Orchard visit: Roma had come from Mozdok, an orphanage three hours from Vladikavkaz, the home of the other Cherry Orchard kids. No explanation was given.

It was like God slipped him in for me.

In early April Kellie got the "Fat Letter" from Carnegie Mellon University, labeled as such as a hint that it was an acceptance letter filled with all the necessary information to enroll. I drove it over to the high school, like a Brinks' truck driver, where she was at a track meet. She celebrated with her friends. My excitement at her being accepted into her first-choice college was tempered by the price tag. The financial award letter would follow.

In a few days that letter revealed that she would be awarded almost $12,000 for her first year. Along with the award document came a letter stating that if we were dissatisfied with the scholarship, we could appeal by submitting the enclosed form. We did, and within a week, received a new award package offering her an additional $4,000 per year renewable scholarship, with another letter. They wrote that if she received more financial aid from comparable universities, to fax them those letters, and they would reconsider her case. We did, and again within a week, she got another $4,000 per year renewable scholarship. The money had far exceeded our expectations. She had received $20,000 for her first year of college. Heather's scholarship amount at Maryland Institute was equivalent. That concern was no longer a worry for our family.

Frank Adoption Center had told us that we would probably leave for Russia sometime in April. Once a court date was set in Moscow, we wouldn't have much notice, maybe less than a week. We had no input about the scheduling. April was a full month already, without squeezing in a trip to Russia!

The first weekend we went to North Carolina for Easter and Spring Break. The second weekend, April 5 –7, Kellie was going on a spiritual retreat for teenagers that was affiliated with my Emmaus ("Faith is adopting an Orphan") retreat. I wanted to be available to hear if her weekend was as life-changing for her as mine had been for me! We were taking Kellie to a "Sleeping Bag" weekend at Carnegie Mellon April 14–15 to help her to make her final college decision. Her eighteenth birthday was April 19. I didn't want to miss that. Taylor was going through Confirmation at church, and Bruce was a mentor for another confirmand. The confirmation party was on May 2. And Kellie was being honored by the Kiwanis Club for being a Teenager of the Year nominee on May 9. If we left in late April, we might miss that. It was going to be difficult to dodge all of these significant events in the lives of my family members.

On April 12, Sharon called to tell us our court date was on April 25. We would fly to Russia April 22, and return May 1. The trip fit right in between all of our scheduled mayhem. We would not miss a single one of our anticipated events.

Our cup runneth over. Our family was experiencing a multitude of miracles!

The prayers our church family offered to God on our behalf, along with the love they showered upon us, had been effective every step of the way. Our last Sunday school class before we left for Russia was saturated with prayer and love. Our dear friends, Jim and Cindy, had tried to transfer Frequent Flyer Miles to us for our plane tickets. When that was unsuccessful, Jim, who works for Marriott, talked to his manager to get us an excellent rate at the Marriott Grand. The Grand was one of the most exclusive hotels in Moscow. It was a five star hotel that cost $300 per night for its cheapest rooms, and up to $600 for the prime suites. Their best rate to adoptive families was $149 per night. Jim got both nights that we were scheduled to stay for $69 per night. Frank Adoption Center could not believe our deal.

One couple gave us a card with a hundred dollars in cash—such a touching and unexpected gift. Another friend slipped me a distinct coin to carry for protection on our journey. I felt encircled with God's love through His people.

I was on a high.

Chapter Eighteen

*"For I know the plans I have for you, declares
the Lord, plans to prosper you and not to harm
you, plans to give you hope and a future."*

Jeremiah 29:11 (NIV)

All along this journey of faith, we had only been capable of taking one small step at a time, but the last step was a leap, a giant hurdle over an ocean and a continent!

The Aeroflot jet that carried us from Washington Dulles International to Moscow International via New York Kennedy Airport was old, but the pilot and crew were efficient and cordial. During the long, dreamlike flight through the shortened night, I could not help but wonder if they considered Americans cold and self-absorbed, their former adversaries they shuttled to the former Soviet Union every day. Jesus said people would recognize his disciples if we loved one another. I made an extra effort to smile and be thankful for everything the crew did. I wanted them to think we were different; I wanted to be ambassadors of Christ to our new ... "cousins," these relatives of my new son.

We landed in Moscow on Tuesday, April 23, late morning, twelve hours and eight time zones from the relative safety of the United States of America.

Once we got off the plane, the competent, English speaking crew scattered, and we began the slow, tedious exodus through customs. I suddenly felt isolated from other English-speaking travelers even though we were shoulder to shoulder with thousands of people. The mass of humanity moved like slow lava to the few open turnstiles where we would declare our valuables, particularly our video camera and the $5000 in cash we were required to bring. Though it made me nervous to disclose we were carrying so much cash, we were instructed to do so because if we were stopped while in Russia and were found to have so much undeclared currency, the officials would deduce that we were involved with contraband and our money could be confiscated. I held it close to my body, under my clothes at all times.

The journey to the turnstile lasted about an hour and a half. We had been instructed before we left to be patient. Once on the other side, we saw our driver holding a "Mr. Michael" sign straight ahead of us. The hour ride to our hotel was surreal, maybe because we hadn't slept in over twenty-four hours, and it would be another ten hours before we had the opportunity to sleep again.

Russia! The mere word conjured up images of spy movies, espionage, and daunting legacies of the Soviet era.

During World War II, Winston Churchill had characterized Russia as "a riddle wrapped in a mystery inside an enigma." I was acutely aware that I was in a vastly different country, nothing like the other European countries where I had traveled.

The buildings we sped past were labeled with that mysterious Cyrillic alphabet. We checked into our hotel, the Marriott Tverskaya, where we would spend one night. Their discount rate to adoptive families was half-price at $149. It was relatively new and sparkling clean. It boasted a terrific breakfast buffet of American favorites, free to families who were adopting. There was no danger of unsafe drinking water at the American hotels in Moscow. In seven days, we would conclude our stay in Moscow at the Marriott Grand, just down the street, for the last two nights. Until then, nine days stretched before me like a medieval pilgrimage. I already ached for my children left behind. What must they be thinking? The girls would be fine, but Taylor was only weeks away from his thirteenth birthday. He was still a child who needed his parents. I knew my neighbors would provide for his needs, and Kellie was with him. Still, I couldn't help worrying about him.

After we had registered at our hotel, we immediately took off down the street for the Kremlin and Red Square, both within walking distance.

Moscow, the capital and largest city of Russia, lies on the Moscow River in the center of western European Russia. It is the country's principle political, cultural, and economic center. Russian emperors, or czars, ruled from Moscow until 1712, when the capital was moved to Saint Petersburg. In 1918, Moscow was restored as the capital, and in 1922, became the capital of the Union of Soviet Socialist Republics until the fall of communism in 1991.

To my surprise, modern-day Moscow appeared to be like any big city. Big name designer stores lined the streets, and some, surprisingly, were labeled in English. There was black dust on everything, but streets were noticeably free of litter. Everywhere workers were sweeping sidewalks and curbs. Because of the fast and profuse traffic, crossing the street was a suicide mission. At every intersection, stairs led down to the city's underground subway system that bustled with activity. The first line of Moscow's metro was completed in 1935, and though extended to serve most of the inner city, it was at present, crowded and insufficient for the volume of travelers. The metro was once known for its ornate stations decorated with statues, stained glass, marble, and chandeliers. By 2002, the stations looked worn and dirty.

The new-rich of Moscow dressed in expensive business suits and chattered away on cell phones. Beautiful women dressed in high fashion down to their stylish ultra-high-heeled, uncomfortable-looking, pointed-toed shoes. My sister Weegie would have said that those shoes' only purpose was for "killing cock roaches in corners."

I smiled, looking down at my own frumpish, sensible shoes covered with the black dust from the sidewalks, as I remembered my sister. I knew that she was thinking of me on the other side of the world.

I was surprised by the crowds of people on a Tuesday afternoon at 3:00. Glitzy shops and arcades were plentiful in these dank catacombs, as were the poor, dirty, young mothers with expressionless babies, begging with a bowl. I wondered how long before those babies too would be relinquished to orphanages.

Situated on the northern bank of the Moscow River, in the heart of Moscow, was the triangular-shaped medieval fortress, the Kremlin. The crisp yellow and white structure inside the wall was spectacularly beautiful with not a trace of the black grime that we had seen on the mile walk there. The self-contained city with a multitude of churches, armories, and palaces had survived within the safety of the stone walls for hundreds of years. The complex was almost one and a half miles in circumference surrounded by stone walls reaching sixty-six feet high. Entering the massive gates into Red Square was like walking into a history lesson. From films, I remembered stone-faced communist leaders marching in the bitter cold, parading their military might in this profoundly daunting space. Along one side of Red Square was Vladimir Lenin's stark Mausoleum, which contained the embalmed remains of the first Soviet leader. Along the opposite side of Red Square was the expansive facade of the world famous department store known as GUM (Russian acronym for State Department Store), which was transferred to private ownership in the early 1990s, after the fall of communism.

Red square is over 400 feet wide and a half a mile long. I stopped and stared often, trying to take a permanent picture of the scene, trying to capture it forever in my mind's eye. At the far end stood the fabled Cathedral of Saint Basil the Blessed. I gasped when I saw it. As we approached the whimsical structure, I gaped like the unabashed tourist that I was, struggling to take in the reality of my physical presence in this legendary place. Perhaps prophetically, the year Roma was born, I had bought Heather and Kellie a puzzle imprinted with its photo. St. Basil's had long fascinated me as an artist. It was built in the sixteenth century to celebrate the military conquests of Ivan the Terrible. The forgotten architect showcased his considerable talent, as did the artisans who had laid the complex brickwork and fabricated the incredible, multicolored onion-top spires. Upon its completion, historians claim that Ivan blinded the architect to prevent him from designing another cathedral as magnificent as St. Basil's.

In 1932 Communist dictator Joseph Stalin ordered St. Basil destroyed because it stood in the way of his military parades. A local architect threatened to cut his own throat on the steps of the cathedral and advocated that the church be made into a museum. Stalin accepted, but the architect spent five years in the gulag for his courage.

I had never in my life expected to be standing in Red Square. On this sunny late afternoon in April, I felt like a speck in the universe.

The next morning, Wednesday, our driver and translator arrived to whisk us away to the domestic airport at promptly 9 a.m. We would travel south, three hours by air to Vladikavkaz. We stopped by another hotel to pick up our traveling companions, an Irish couple, Geraldine and Tom. They were adopting a two-year-old boy from the same region. The four of us would be together throughout our stay in Vladikavkaz. We enjoyed having another couple with which to share our excitement.

The domestic airport was nothing like the grand Moscow International Airport. The familiar and ominous hammer and sickle still branded the front of the long, flat building. There had been few updated features for this facility over the years. When we asked about a restroom, we were directed to the roofless cinderblock structure out back. Once there, Geraldine and I discovered only holes in the ground over which we stood, and no place to wash our hands.

The plane was old, but the flight was smooth. I still had moments of uncertainty. It was a sick feeling; more turbulence in my troubled waters. But one day was down, and in only eight more, we could go home. I would deal with my fears on familiar ground.

As we neared our destination, still above the cloud cover, I saw a strange sight along the horizon.

"Are those mountains?" I asked slowly, in disbelief.

"Noooo!" my scientist husband answered, not believing that I had asked such a ridiculous question.

I did feel rather silly for asking. The sight was like nothing I had previously seen.

We studied in silence the jagged white clouds rising high above the other flat clouds. I trusted my husband's answer; I was no scientist. I watched him continue to scrutinize the spectacle.

"Those are mountains," he said slowly, almost in disbelief, embarrassed for having dismissed my question so abruptly. The snow-capped peaks reached high above the clouds. During our descent, we closed in on the Alp-like setting. We inquired and learned that we were approaching an area in the Caucasus Mountains. I remembered from my interest in geography that Mount Elbrus, the highest mountain in Europe at over 18,000 feet, was in western Russia and was part of the Caucasus Mountains. During all my preparations for our trip to Russia, I had failed to be curious about where we would travel—I had bigger concerns than our physical destination. The beauty took my breath. I had not expected it.

Our new drivers and translator met us at the airport and packed us all into two small, black, antiquated and decrepit Russian-made cars. The "Ladas" resembled boxy, tinny, Japanese Datsun B210s that many of my friends drove during my high school years in the 1970s.

Our guide and translator, Elena, educated us about her lovely hometown. Vladikavkaz was the capital of the Republic of North Ossetia-Alania, part of North Caucasia, a country of three-quarters of a million people. To the south lay the Republic of Georgia, to the east, war-torn Chechnya.

We drove forty to fifty minutes through rural countryside, occasionally slowing to drive around a cow standing in the road. One car was packed beyond capacity with Geraldine and Tom, the region coordinator, their driver, and luggage. Our translator Elena, our driver Solz, Bruce and I followed closely in the other, holding suitcases on our laps. There were no seat belts. I wondered how each car would hold an extra child after our court date. I remembered that each of our families had brought an extra suitcase filled with gifts for the orphanage that we would leave behind. That would make room.

We finally pulled into the red, muddy, unpaved parking lot of the apartment complex. Geraldine and Tom had warned us that, at first sight, the apartment building looked like a slum. They assured us that once inside, the residence was remarkably clean and quite comfortable. They had visited their baby, David, three weeks earlier and had stayed with the same host family. The new law for Russian adoptions required two separate visits. Because Roma had visited with us in November, and he knew us, the embassy waived our second visit.

I was glad that I was somewhat prepared for the condition of the building. The shabby elevator shuddered to a stop, and Geraldine and I boarded with our luggage. There was only room for the two of us. As the doors creaked slowly closed, I saw Bruce on the other side through the gap in the doors that didn't quite meet. I thought for the first time that maybe I should be frightened.

When the front door opened to the sunny little apartment, I was relieved. The smell of cooked cabbage wafted from the warm kitchen beside the front hall. Svetlana met us at the door. She was a pleasant, petite young woman about thirty years old. She spoke no English except for a few welcoming phases she had learned to greet her guests. She shared the flat with her husband, who turned out to be Solz, our driver. Elena, our translator, along with the veteran visitors, Geraldine and Tom, filled us in on the details of our hosts. Svetlana's mother was the administrator at the baby orphanage where little David lived. We learned that Svetlana was a psychologist, and Solz, a policeman, each earning about $30 a month. The money they earned by hosting Americans and Europeans who were adopting, for the use of their apartment, preparing meals, and taxiing, was much more lucrative than their regular jobs. Thus, they could afford their apartment, for which they had paid $10,000 to own. They cooked and cleaned for us, then left every evening to stay at the home of Svetlana's mother. We stayed there three days and nights.

The large windows were filled with the incredible Caucasus Mountains. If not for the blatant poverty of the shacks that nestled at the base of the mountains, I could easily have imagined that we were staying at a popular Alpine resort. Geraldine and Tom said that when they had visited three weeks before, clouds had obscured the mountains. We marveled at the beauty together.

The apartment was immaculate, and the food was superb. Delicious soups, fresh vegetables, and even meat (though I dared not ask what kind of meat) were beautifully served on lovely china. It was easy to forget that we were not staying in a five-star bed and breakfast. After dinner, Tanya, Elena, and our gracious hosts left for the evening, and we stayed up talking into the wee hours of the morning with our new friends.

At daybreak on Wednesday, I was wide awake. The snow on the mountains reflected the bright pink of the early sun. The entire back wall of the apartment was windows. A door opened onto a narrow porch where I could sit outside in the crisp morning air and wonder what in the world I was doing so far from home, sharing the apartment of strangers with more strangers, for the purpose of adopting a child who didn't even speak my language. A familiar melancholy was creeping back.

To our surprise, Roma was delivered to our door about 9 a.m., wearing that same worn, brown sweater and baggy blue jeans that he wore the first time I laid anxious eyes on him in a church basement in Frederick, Maryland. That seemed like years ago. I couldn't help but wonder what had happened to the new clothes I had bought him last November. His new Nike sneakers, Pokémon shirt, and red down vest had been a source of enormous pride for him. I imagined the other children at the orphanage were wearing Roma's clothes at that moment. I was pleased that another child might have a reason for joy as Roma had, and sad that I had not done more. The one suitcase I had packed for Roma's orphanage didn't hold nearly enough.

The same backpack that I had sent back to Russia with him was packed neatly with his toothpaste, toothbrush, comb, soap, underwear, a pair of girls tights, a full change of clothes, and a lovely lavender jacket with ruffles around the hood. The clothes were probably donations to the orphanage. I was thankful that I had shopped for Roma before we left the States. We had been prepared for him to arrive with nothing but the clothes he was wearing.

We had not anticipated seeing him until the court case the following day. Elena, having talked to his driver, related the story that Roma was the hero at his orphanage. He was the first child ever to be adopted from the Mozdok Home for Children. Where was Mozdok? Elena explained that Mozdok was close to Chechnya where fierce fighting was common. American civilians were not permitted to travel to a war zone, so an employee of the Mozdok Home had driven Roma to us, a sixty mile distance that had taken three hours. He had left the orphanage at 6 a.m.

Roma was awkward with us and nervously raced through the apartment. He made friends quickly with Elena, Svetlana and Solz. Svetlana had met him days before to evaluate him for the adoption in her capacity as a psychologist. As he had been with his compatriots during their visit to Maryland in November, Roma was perfectly comfortable with the Russian adults. He laughed with them. He was funny. Sometimes they would share a story. Elena told us that when he went to America, he wanted a new name: Arthur. We all wondered why that name would appeal to a seven-year-old boy.

Roma was even friendly to Geraldine and Tom, but he would not even look at Bruce and me. We had brought a few toys with us, but he was not interested. He had been comfortable with us before, but now in the role as a new son, he was going to be cautious. We had not earned his trust as "Mama and Papa." His last mama and papa had let him down. He was a shrewd little guy; he was not going to get hurt again. We would have to be patient and earn his trust.

He would be staying with us in the apartment, even though we didn't go to court to legally adopt him until Thursday afternoon. Geraldine and Tom's baby, David, would stay in the baby orphanage in Vladikavkaz until Saturday morning when we left for the airport. The apartment could not accommodate the needs of a two-year-old.

Later on Wednesday morning, we all went to visit David at his orphanage. The rooms and play areas were brightly colored and spotless. The few toys were mended and clean. The caregivers were loving and attentive, but there were too few of them. It was heartbreaking to see four or five infants lying in a crib, unable to turn themselves over or even to raise their heads.

"How old are they?" I asked, expecting to hear about three to six months, according to their size and motor skills.

Twelve to fifteen months was the shocking answer. The women who took care of so many abandoned babies were doing their best, but the job was overwhelming.

My previous ambivalence over adopting returned in waves. Was this more of the dangerous, white-water rapids approaching another steep fall? So far, I had been pushed along at the mercy of the current. I had surrendered to God's leading and had given up having a say in the direction of the course. At times I was very happy to have this little boy with us. At other times, I was keenly aware that I had signed no legal documents, and the official adoption had not yet been decreed. I still had time to change my mind.

On Thursday morning we visited another Vladikavkaz orphanage for older children. It was the home of the children and principal from the previous November's Cherry Orchard Program. Rita, the principal, greeted us on the steps with a warm hug. A group of boys was entering the building as we arrived, many wearing threadbare wool coats. I felt part of a Charles Dickens story. Roma's friend from November's visit, Yevgeniy, was among then. I was so excited to see him, I called out his name, smiling. He looked at us, and then at Roma, and his sad, mature eyes revealed his painful realization—we had come for Roma, but no one had come for him. He was trying to be hospitable, as Rita spoke softly to him in Russian.

I thought again of Charles Dickens. In his 1861 novel, *Great Expectations,* about a young orphan, he wrote, "In the little world in which children exist, there is nothing so finely perceived and so finely felt as injustice." Dickens would have understood Yevgeniy feelings. I understood, too, and that moment was the saddest of our journey.

Maybe Roma understood too. Or, he was afraid of being left behind at another orphanage. He raced back to the car to wait out our visit by Solz's side. Solz was a tremendous hit with Roma because he let Roma push the buttons on his car radio.

We toured Rita's school, just as she and her compatriots had toured the American school. It was a much shorter tour, but she was equally proud of her school. We were impressed that even with limited funds, they had created an atmosphere of learning and respect for others and for themselves. She led us into a class in session. Upon our entering, the students immediately stood by their seats out of respect for their principal, and maybe for us, too. The teacher explained to them that we were visiting Americans. I hoped the children didn't think we had come seeking a child to adopt. They were on their best behavior. Coming from a school environment, I grimaced to think that our own privileged, pampered students were not nearly this respectful, nor this eager to learn! The teacher called on a pretty girl about twelve, who came up to the world map that still identified the vast eastern part of the map as "CCCP". She did as she was obviously instructed and pointed to the United States with a smile that could rival an angel's. I wondered how many American students could point to Russia on a world map.

We joined Rita in her office for tea and cookies after the tour. Elena translated for us. Rita said she was surprised to see us; she had thought she would never see us again. Apparently Roma had made quite an impression on her. She had been responsible for him for twelve hours on a plane each way and for getting him to and from the airports, as well as all the waiting in between. I knew that Roma was not a patient child! Plus, Rita shared that Roma had stayed with them at the Vladikavkaz Home for a couple of days before they left for the United States. Obviously she had been with him long enough to form an enduring impression of his energy level!

I had thought until our arrival in Vladikavkaz that this was Roma's home, too, that he and Yevgeniy had been friends for the two years that Roma had been in the Children's Home. But Roma's friendship with Yevgeniy was brand new as of the November trip. Someone had to have made a decision to drive Roma three hours from Mozdok to Vladikavkaz before his trip to America in November, just as he had been delivered to us at Svetlana's apartment on Wednesday. Why Roma? Vladikavkaz seemed to have plenty of its own children in need of families.

I could imagine God tapping His chin and pondering, "Roma, Roma, Roma . . . ? Hmmm . . ." And then the best possible answer: "Ah yes, the Michaels in Mount Airy, Maryland."

In the afternoon we visited a small zoo, with a few animals. A camel, some elk, two or three reindeer, some wolves, and several exotic-looking birds were the extent of the wild life at the Vladikavkaz Zoo. Roma enjoyed playing on a small statue of a gorilla more than looking at the animals. He remained distant from Bruce and me, and sweetly affectionate to everyone else, even to Geraldine and Tom. It was as if he was saying, "See how lovable I can be, but I'm not so sure about you yet."

I didn't want to pressure him, so I almost went too far the other way. I almost ignored him. I was unsure about how to bridge the distance between us. If I was unsure, I couldn't imagine how confused Roma must be.

On Thursday we toured Vladikavkaz. We walked around a large cemetery of writers, politicians, artists, musicians, and anyone remotely famous who had lived in Vladikavkaz. We traveled twenty minutes and were deep into the mountains. The temperature was considerably colder. My sweater that had been comfortable the entire trip was no longer sufficient. Elena was clearly proud of her beautiful city in the shadow of breathtaking mountains. She had traveled to Scotland to learn English. She was a high school Russian Literature teacher when she wasn't translating for English speaking visitors to this region. I was in awe of her as I remembered never finishing *War and Peace*, and struggling with every other Tolstoy and Dostoevsky book I had ever attempted but failed to finish. She was intelligent and patient. She took us by her lovely church. Though Easter had passed, it was still the Lenten season in the Eastern Orthodox Church. Elena had given up meat and cigarettes for Lent.

We rushed back to meet Geraldine and Tom for lunch, before we had to change and drive to the courthouse.

Geraldine and Tom's case was first. We waited out in the hall for one hour for our turn in the courtroom while Geraldine and Tom became legal parents of little David. The gentleman who had driven Roma from Mozdok was there to wait with his young ward. I say gentle man because he was. He was a burly man, probably in his forties, heavy set, but he spoke to Roma with such gentleness. I could not comprehend his language, but I understood his compassion. And Roma was noticeably fond of him too.

We entered the stark courtroom as Elena slid into the bench behind us to translate the proceedings. The trial was routine, and much faster than Geraldine and Tom's had been, about fifteen minutes. Bruce answered a few questions that we were expecting: how long we had been married; did we own our home; how many other children did we have; and how did our other children feel about adopting? Then the matronly judge looked at us and spoke about the sadness that the Russian people felt in losing their children. But she said that they must think of the children's best interest. The petition for adoption was granted. Although the proceedings had a monumental impact on my life, the case itself seemed mundane.

We returned to the hallway where Geraldine and Tom, Tanya, Roma, and his driver waited. I never knew his name, but after the trial, the gentleman spoke softly to our remarkably quiet and attentive new son. Maybe serious advice for a happy and successful life was being imparted. He pulled a small, clear plastic horse head, perhaps a chess piece, out of his pocket. It was a toy I might have treasured as a child. Roma was familiar with this toy and was excited to take it. When the man stood up, he tousled Roma's hair. Then he took his handkerchief out of his pocket and wiped tears from his own eyes. Such tenderness brought a fresh flood of tears to my own eyes. Bruce was tearfully speechless, also.

We stepped out into the afternoon sunshine and took group pictures. Then I watched this man return to his car for his three-hour trip back to Mozdok. Another adult had disappeared from Roma's life forever. It was a wonder that he was not fearful of creating new bonds. Though he was presently testing Bruce and me, he seemed to bond easily and appropriately with all the other adults I had ever seen him encounter. He was mischievously playful with all of them, not shy with a one.

When we returned to the apartment with our new son, I was overwhelmed and panic-stricken. We had ten days to change our minds before the adoption decree became official, and don't think I didn't contemplate what everyone's reaction would be if we returned home without the boy! I wondered if that had ever happened before.

Tom had bought a bottle of champagne to celebrate. Aware that alcohol is a depressant, I declined a drink, fearing my fragile mood. Celebration did not coincide with the state of my nerves that evening.

My journey of two years had taken me through a series of rough cascades, followed by smooth sailing, and then again, through dangerous rapids. The Niagara Falls-sized plunge for which I had braced myself for two years had finally begun on the plane to Russia. Even while sitting among these lovely Russian and Irish people and my new son who was yet a stranger to me, I still had the sensation of free-falling. Down, down, down, I plummeted, not knowing when or how I would hit bottom. I was terrified by the prospect of what lay at the bottom of this fall that I had been approaching for two years. I had been powerless to prevent the progression toward the point of no return. I had anticipated the plunging waters long before I arrived on the brink. I had tried to choose a safe escape, but the current swept me down the rapids closer to the abyss that I seemed now to face. I had done it, convinced my family that we needed to adopt a child from Russia, traveled half way around the world, and signed the papers. What now?

Again, I remembered the up and down pattern of the Jewish people in the Old Testament, of doing what was right in the sight of the Lord and flourishing, alternating with turning away from the Lord, and suffering the consequences.

The sick, doubting feeling was not totally a surprise; it had been a regular visitor for two years. But my sudden ambivalent feeling toward Bruce was not expected. Suddenly everything he said and did annoyed me. He seemed to be saying stupid things in front of our new friends, Geraldine and Tom. I was cranky and irritated that he was in a celebratory mood with these happy new parents. He didn't notice my feelings. Here we were, in an unfamiliar country, sharing the home of foreigners with complete strangers. Why hadn't Bruce stopped me; why did he let this happen? It was terrifying to realize that we had put our happy life in jeopardy. Many marriages didn't withstand this kind of monumental disruption. Would we be able to overcome the challenges?

The story of our beginning as a couple has always been precious to me. I hold it close and carefully like a fragile gift. It is the movie of my life that I rewind and watch over and over because it is so romantic and beautiful. If our marriage failed, that perfect and at times heartbreaking story of our inception would be null and void with no reason to retell it or even to remember it. If we disintegrated as a couple, it would diminish the importance of that magical age of youthful love and everything that had transpired since. On the roller coaster that is marriage, Bruce and I had mostly enjoyed the moments that make you want to keep riding. Any of the "valleys" came from some smallness in me, some feeling of insecurity or inadequacy.

Bruce was such a good man, the same man who, at twenty-one years of age had bowled me over when I was a college freshman. I remembered it like . . . like it was a couple of years ago instead of twenty-seven . . .

Chapter Nineteen

"I have found the paradox, that if
you love until it hurts, there can be
no more hurt, only more love."

Mother Teresa

I first laid hopeful eyes on Bruce Michael a few minutes past three o'clock on the afternoon of January 20, 1975, on the campus of North Carolina State University.

The first day of spring semester, I dutifully showed up for badminton class, a P.E. credit that consisted of seventeen boys and three girls. My friends considered me a flirt; I liked to think of myself as "playful." Whatever label fit, I liked the odds.

I saw him and listened for his name during roll call. Our teacher, Mr. Cheek, paired us up as opponents just as I was falling for him.

I went back to my dorm room talking about the guy in my badminton class. With the help of the school directory, I learned where his apartment was off campus, his phone number, and that he was a junior from Fairfax, Virginia. With the anonymity that pre-Caller ID afforded me, I boldly called his apartment just to hear his voice, but then I panicked and hung up. The voice I'd wanted to hear struck me dumb—both verbally and intellectually. I covertly rode by his apartment. I was beginning to resemble a stalker, but I was stalking *subtly*. My mother taught me that nice girls don't chase boys, and the best approach with boys was to play hard-to-get.

I was utterly fascinated by him. He possessed a humble confidence I had not known in other boys I had dated. He was friendly, but not flirtatious, which annoyed me at first. The next few classes, I arrived early in hopes that we would talk before class. Then one day he didn't show up. It was in that class, during the gentleman's game of badminton, hardly a physical-contact sport, I almost broke my arm. I fell backwards, landed on my hand, and bent my elbow the wrong way. The next class, February 10, I went with my black and blue arm in a crisp, new sling from the infirmary to tell Mr. Cheek about my hyper-extended elbow. I really went to show Bruce my injury and, perhaps, to garner some sympathy. He was there on crutches. He had come to tell Mr. Cheek that he too would be unable to play for a week. He had sprained his ankle while playing basketball with friends. We stood beside the court talking long after our classmates began chasing shuttlecocks. Eventually, we started walking back toward my dorm and his car. When we got to where our destinations split, we stopped again and talked. Finally he said, "What's your phone number? Maybe I'll call you sometime."

Dumbstruck, I paused too long to remember my number.

"Orrr . . . maybe I won't" he said, thinking that I was putting him off.

I recovered and gave him the number. He wrote it on the cover of the notebook he was carrying. "And what is your name?" he asked, poised to write it above my number.

My usually confident ego suffered a humbling blow. How ironic that in those three weeks, I had resorted to spy tactics to discover personal data about him, and he didn't even know my name!

Floating into my suite of five rooms and nine other suitemates, I babbled about the afternoon, my lucky injury, and Bruce. I had talked about him for three weeks straight but with no reciprocation or encouragement on his part, until now.

"What about John?" Betsy, my roommate, asked soberly.

I guess this is an appropriate time to mention that I already had a boyfriend. John was not a faded, high-school boyfriend soon to be kicked to the curb like so many victims of college freshmen in a new pool of prospects. He *was* the new boyfriend. I had gone home at Christmas to dismiss my comfortable high-school boyfriend, so I wouldn't feel guilty about dating John. The first day of the semester I had met Bruce, and my fickle response to Betsy was almost "John who?" This was a pattern for me. The chase had always been the most exciting part of the relationship.

Bruce's name was still on my lips when he phoned. He was going to be on campus for a botany test that evening, and would I like to go out afterwards? I would worry about John later. John lived on the second floor of my twelve-story, coed dorm. I lived in the "pent house" of Metcalf Dorm.

At about 7:00, when I was expecting Bruce, John came through my open door. I was pretending to study at my desk and didn't encourage him to stay. He was just looking for notes from calculus to borrow, he said, sensing my unwelcoming attitude. Betsy gave him her notes and hurried him out. Bruce came moments later. They probably passed at the elevator!

We went to Darryl's, an eclectic bar across Hillsborough Street. Bruce ordered a pitcher of dark beer; I had a coke.

This became our regular schedule. We played badminton on Monday and Wednesday afternoons in class, and went out on Monday nights, while Bruce was conveniently on campus for his Monday night botany tests. No phone calls to chat, no weekend dates. Sometimes he would ask beforehand, after badminton, sometimes he would just show up at my room after his botany class. It was impossible to judge his interest in me.

On those Monday nights when we did get together, I would sit across from him, mesmerized, as he related his adventures: hitch-hiking to California and Nova Scotia, sky diving, scuba diving in the Florida Keys, canoeing in alligator-infested rivers in Georgia. And he was only twenty-one. I had barely left the state of North

Carolina, except for summer trips to Myrtle Beach! I let him do most of the talking. My stories didn't compare to his, but I was an attentive listener! I finally told John about Bruce, although I could hardly call our Monday night jaunts "dates." They more resembled platonic hangouts. Even so, I wanted to discourage an exclusive relationship with John. I did not mention John to Bruce. Often after Bruce would bring me home, John would show up and want to have serious talks about "us." Betsy was sprouting gray hairs because of my love-triangle escapades! In the following weeks, I learned that the chase was the fun part of relationships for John, too. I was very much a challenge, now that Bruce had entered the scene. And suddenly John was determined to win me over. John had been a fun chase, but the challenge was about over for me. The more he held on, the more desperate he became, and the less attractive he was to me. But I wasn't confident about Bruce and whether this relationship would go forward. John was fun. He was a flirt. A suitemate had a serious crush on John which made him a little more attractive to me, so I didn't dismiss him entirely.

After five weeks of going to Darryl's every Monday night together, Bruce kissed me when he left. It was not an "I'm crazy about you" kiss, but it wasn't a kiss he would give a little sister either. For me, it changed everything. John pleaded with me not to see Bruce anymore; however, in his desperation, John was no longer attractive to me. For the first time, I became aware of my immaturity in relationships. I wondered if Bruce was not such a hard one to read or win, would I be so consumed with adoration. Bruce was proving my mother's advice about playing-hard-to-get was accurate. I just wanted him to be crazy about me, then maybe I could move on to the next challenge. Bruce wouldn't give me that opportunity!

He was remarkably different from anyone I had ever known. He was intelligent, gentle and strong. I had gone out with boys; Bruce was a man. He was a motivated intellectual who seemed to know what he wanted from life. He wanted to make a difference in the world. I feared he was too busy preparing for life to need me to be part of it. He liked me, but Bruce seemed to like everyone. When Bruce would visit, several of my suitemates would drop in and line up on our beds to talk to him. He was an attraction.

"He looks like Jesus," one of my suitemates observed one evening. His hair was shoulder length, like so many guys wore it in the 1970s. He had a beautiful complexion and high, rosy cheeks and he had a beard. (I had never dated a guy who could grow a beard!) Beyond his resemblance to Jesus, his blue eyes weaken me. I was euphoric when I thought Bruce might care for me. I was miserable when I couldn't maintain that hope. I was completely and miserably in love. Heartsick confusion was a new emotion for me. Usually before I ever got to this state, the boy would have declared his undying love and turned me off. Bruce was not even giving me a clue. I was losing control.

We started seeing more of each other on some weekends, but he never invited me to his apartment, and he only introduced me to his friends if we ran into them when we were around campus. He never called just to talk. He didn't seem to find me irresistible. When May came and everyone headed home for the summer, I cheerfully wished him a happy summer. I never wanted Bruce to know how lost I felt in leaving him for three months. His home was five hours away, so I didn't expect to see him during our break. I played it cool, not wanting to appear to be a high-maintenance girlfriend. I wasn't even sure I *was* his girlfriend.

We wrote friendly and generic letters during the summer. I called him once to tell him something I thought was important at the time, mainly to hear his voice and remind him about me.

I could not wait for summer to be over. My mother remarried during that summer of 1975. As happy as I was for her, and as much as we all loved Nathan, my mood was already fragile from longing for Bruce's love. We moved across town to Nathan's much nicer home and away from the apartment where I had spent twelve years growing up. Had I been in a better frame of mind and not relationally confused and self-absorbed, I would have welcomed the change in the life and security of my mother. But I moped all summer, afraid to be hopeful about love.

In August, I went back to Raleigh four days early because Bruce's letter revealed that he was returning then. A friend drove me to his apartment where we found him unloading his car. He was friendly to us but never invited us in. My hopes plummeted when he was so casual with me. Things were awkward. I regretted that we had stopped by, as my mother's advice, "Don't chase boys," echoed in my mind.

Weeks would pass without me seeing him, and then out of the blue, he would stop by while he was on campus, just for a casual visit. In October he asked me to the celebrated State-Carolina football game. Although Betsy warned me not to get my hopes up, cautious optimism inflated my spirit. Every time I would get encouraged, Betsy suffered with me when those hopes were shattered. As usual, Betsy was right; nothing magical happened. In December, right before Christmas break, during one of his spontaneous visits, we sat alone in my room. He sat on Betsy's bed while I faced him on mine, four feet across our small room. Linda Ronstadt sang on the radio. Suddenly I heard her song more than Bruce's empty words:

"I've done everything I know, to try and make you mine, and I think it's gonna hurt me for a long, long time," she crooned.

The smile that I always tried to wear when he visited unexpectedly turned to painful tears. I could not control myself. He moved to my side, surprised. "Debbie, what's wrong?" He tried to comfort me, but he didn't have a clue.

I went home for Christmas break, determined to get over him.

Nineteen seventy-six was a year of celebrating national history. I wanted to celebrate a new beginning. Every time I felt like I was making progress in moving beyond Bruce, he would stop by to visit. I considered asking him to stop coming, but I was afraid he would comply. Instead, I would be friendly when he came, and fall apart after he was gone.

I dated others, even returning to John briefly, and as expected, none measured up to Bruce. I saw him afar occasionally with another girl around campus. The pain of that made me want to leave school. One day I found myself walking behind them from class. Not seeing me, they stopped in my path, talking. Her flirtatious manner made my heart ache. She was obviously crazy about him. As I passed them, he saw me and tried to engage me in the conversation. It was all I could do to be pleasant and keep walking. I knew I would have time for a good cry, if I could just make it back to my room, and Betsy. She loved me like a sister, and comforted me like no one else. I had a couple of close guy pals who tried to advise me too. Howard naively suggested I tell Bruce that I was pregnant, to force his hand; however, my relationship with Bruce had never been complicated with sex.

That semester I took a poetry writing class. All of my raw disappointment and frustration found a voice. I remember our instructor, Lance Jeffers, asked if he could see me after class one day. I stayed and he asked about my poetry, "so full of love and pain." I never wrote the words "love" or "pain," though the emotions were always just below the surface. My poems were merely a series of images, no rhyming involved, that left the reader with a lost hopelessness. I was satisfied with their account of my feelings. I was pleased that Lance felt the love and pain throbbing between the lines. When I revealed I was also a visual artist, he said he should have known—through poetry, I was painting with words instead of paint.

Spring is my favorite season in North Carolina. The tender green leaves are emerging, and rebirth, revitalization, and hope seem to sprout with the flowers. Even my poems that spring sounded more hopeful. I revisited the idea that just maybe . . . maybe I still had a chance with Bruce. Most days I was realistic, knowing I would probably live though this heartbreak. I was determined. But the music I chose was torture. Joan Baez's heartrending "Diamonds and Rust" always left me in an abysmal funk.

> "Well I'll be damned,
> Here comes your ghost again,
> But that's not unusual,
> It's just that the moon is full and
> You happen to call.
> And here I sit,
> Hand on a telephone,
> Hearing a voice I'd known,
> a couple of light years ago,
> Heading straight for a fall."

(I still can't listen to that song without being snatched back to 1976 and a vivid memory of having my heart ripped out!)

I lived for my poetry. It was therapeutic. It was my way to communicate with Bruce. Strings of words almost involuntarily wove together to create concrete images in my mind, and they appeared so suddenly sometimes I would have to search for a scrap of paper, to record them before they dissipated. I could be in a chemistry lecture or driving down the highway when a phrase or image came to me. Sometimes I had to pull off the road and write down the fleeting string of words that was worth a thousand pictures.

The dark auditorium of my chemistry class became a sanctuary of brilliant inspiration. I sat in the back and daydreamed as phrases of poetry connected themselves into satisfying self-assessments, ignoring equations on a faraway screen. On the last day to drop a class, I withdrew from chemistry with a fifty-four average. I didn't need chemistry; meteorology would satisfy the science requirement for my major. I was reluctant, however, to give up the environment that had fostered such creativity!

One day in March Bruce stopped by for a rare visit, feeling

lethargic. He was about to graduate in two months and suddenly didn't know what his future held.

"Oh, you'll go to grad school, get a job, and when the time is right, a beautiful wife will appear." I spelled it out for him.

"You are the type my mother would like," he responded, lying on my bed, sighing, as I sat at my desk.

It should have been a compliment, but it didn't feel like one. My heart sank, again, as I realized I was not what he had planned for. However, without leading me on or giving me false hope, he had still nurtured a small ember deep in my soul that he cared about me; otherwise, I would have been capable of moving on. But if he was determined not to give us a chance, I was doomed.

"Here," I said as I picked up my poetry notebook from my desk. I had hidden my feelings from him so successfully. Now I was about to expose my tender heart and my secret love for him. And for what? It really didn't matter anymore, and I knew it would change nothing.

I handed him two newly typed poems. He settled back to read. He paused for a long time when he was finished.

Then he handed them back to me, awkwardly.

"I had no idea," he spoke slowly.

"I know," I answered softly. Our eyes met and I glanced away quickly because I could never look into those eyes again.

When he left, I didn't feel as if I had compromised my position. I had no position. In two months he would be gone. Maybe he would remember me fondly. That was the only hope I could afford.

I would certainly remember him. Forever.

Every year in mid-April, a big campus-wide party was sponsored by the university. "The Day" it was called. My friends and I sat on blankets listening to bands and getting sun burned from morning until late afternoon. About mid-day Bruce stopped by our blanket to say hi. I felt that painful hopefulness rise in me again, but he didn't linger long. His roommate, Lee, later joined us and chatted for a while. I didn't know Lee well. Bruce had only introduced us when we ran into him around campus one day. He came back later and stayed for a while longer. One of Bruce's other roommates, Mike, joined us too. They made our blanket home base, though I didn't see Bruce anymore that day.

That night when we went home, I was talking on the phone with a guy I had met earlier in the day, another attempt at pushing Bruce out of my heart. I was standing in the hall where our common phone was installed, when I looked out of the glass door of our suite and saw Lee rounding the elevator. Lee had come to visit me! I motioned him back to my room and started to say encouraging goodbyes to the boy on the phone. Several minutes later, as I was hanging up the phone, I noticed Bruce's other roommate, Mike, was coming toward our suite door. When Mike followed me back to my room, he and Lee looked embarrassed to see each other. Mike didn't stay long.

Lee stayed for hours. When he left, we made plans to see each other again. I was shameless! I lead him to believe I was interested in him. Maybe Lee was something like Bruce. Maybe he would have to do, in the absence of Bruce.

The next morning I awoke to the reality that Lee was not and never would be Bruce. I was devastated that I might have slammed a door I had left ajar for the last year. I wanted to go back and fling the door open again. The attraction with Lee was merely his connection to his roommate.

I cried all day. Betsy had lived through this with me and saved my sanity many times, but she was ready to resign as my therapist! I was ready to admit defeat.

The next day, Monday, I was ready to start life anew, without Bruce or his replacement. After my last class, I saw Bruce ahead of me in the mass exodus from classes. I always recognized his shape and his gait. He was slow, and at one point turned and saw me. And he waited! My heart pounded as I casually caught up with him. We engaged in the shallow chit-chat I had become so proficient at and detested so vehemently.

Maybe Bruce didn't know about Lee's visit. But as we approached the point where our paths parted, he began, "Lee said he came to see you Saturday night."

We stopped under the magnolia trees in front of Reynolds Coliseum.

"Yeah," was all I wanted to say. I wondered if he knew that Mike had come, too. How odd that both of his roommates had wanted to visit me, but he did not.

"We waited for Lee to come home to go to dinner with us, but he didn't show up," Bruce casually began. "We didn't know where he was. He didn't return all evening. I went to bed before he came in. Last night we asked him where he had been, and he said he had been at Debbie's. I thought he meant another Debbie we knew. But he said no, it was *my* friend Debbie. I got up from the table and threw my plate of spaghetti at the wall on the way out."

This was the most encouraged I had ever been, until he added, "At least it will be easier now." He paused and looked over his shoulder, anywhere so he wouldn't have to look at me.

"Why will it be easier now?" I asked angrily. I continued, "I know, because you are leaving and you have plans."

"It just wouldn't work for us. We are so different," he blurted.

"I guess you are right. And there's nothing I can say to change your mind anyway," I retorted.

We stood in silence. I feared he might turn to leave, as I fought the impulse to protest the injustice. He cared, and I knew it, but that new affirmation would change nothing. The knowledge would only hurt me more! He didn't *want* to care.

I took several deep breaths until I trusted myself to speak slowly and deliberately through my brewing tears. "I'm just . . . so afraid . . . I am always going to feel this way about you."

There was an extended pause in which a few stifled sobs escaped from me. Bruce shifted uncomfortably during the awkward silence.

Finally the wall protecting him from commitment crumbled as he whispered, "In a way I hope you always will."

My sobs shook me. He pulled me close to comfort me. I stood wrapped in his arms, feeling his broken breaths on my face.

"Have dinner with me tonight so we can talk," he said.

After dinner we walked holding hands, as I floated, remembering in amazement how bleakly the day had begun.

"Hello woman of my dreams," Bruce sang along to a distant radio, to Neil Young's "Cowgirl in the Sand," gazing at me with eyes of love I had only dreamed of. The wall was down; he did love me, had loved me all the time, he confessed, but he was afraid to give his heart completely. He was a little afraid of my immaturity in the beginning. Smart guy!

God had given me Bruce, but first He had matured me and made me worthy.

We were married two years later when I graduated.

Over the years, many of my friends have confessed that if they had it to do over, they might not choose their spouses a second time. I know when I look at Bruce playing with our kids, or riding the lawn tractor, or rearranging his wood pile the way men do, he is the only one for me.

Back in Russia, twenty-seven years later, taking a few minutes to reflect on our past, to appreciate the gift of our love and the accomplishment of our long marriage reframed my perspective. When I recognized that the devil was again at work testing my resolve, rattling my nerves, and inciting me to critical hatefulness, I began to get control of my feelings. I had to push Satan's self-serving, spiteful attempt at sabotaging this moment behind me. I realized (serving as my own therapist for once) I was projecting my anxiety at this monumental apex onto Bruce—the one I could always trust not to reject me, no matter how loopy I behaved. Roma was not the only one testing the limits, wondering who to trust. I had my own brief moment of acting out, but once again, Bruce was sure and steady, my rock in Russia as well as at home.

As I reflected on my relationship with Bruce, I could not help but remember a long ago conversation that still echoed in the fringes of my memory. Another piece of the extraordinary adoption puzzle? When the first unwelcome hints of adoption threatened to turn my happy life upside down, I was reminded of something Bruce had said decades ago. During a conversation very early in our relationship, before he loved me, innocently, I had related a study we had read about in psychology class revealing a large percentage of parents surveyed said, if given a chance to do it over, they would rather remain childless. I was shocked by the statistic. I was sure my mother didn't feel that way.

Bruce, who had not realized I had already claimed him as my future husband and father of my children-to-be, made an unsettling observation. "The world is already overcrowded, and there are so many unwanted children, I will probably adopt," he had said, nonchalantly.

We never discussed it again. But adoption was not in *my* future plans; at least that's what I thought at nineteen.

Had this been a casual comment by an idealistic and altruistic young man? Maybe. But perhaps God was planting a seed He would harvest twenty-five years later.

When the adoption issue flared up in 2000, I reminded Bruce about the comment and asked if he had indeed always wanted to adopt. He confessed that he didn't know why he had said it, that he hadn't thought of it in years. But he had *said* it. This statement, like Taylor's comment that he had always wanted a little brother, had spurred me to action, had helped me to accept God's leading. Yet both Bruce and Taylor had spoken with no real conviction or forethought. Had their off-handed remarks been part of God's plan? I began to wonder if *adoption* had been God's design for Bruce and me from the beginning, and if so . . . Wow.

My simple brain was not capable of stretching itself around such a profound concept. My limited consciousness and understanding could not even begin to fathom the complexities of such an immense God and His inspired plans.

Bruce's idealism and "change-the-world" aspirations had endeared him to me in the 1970s. He was my heart's deepest desire. Many times I have thanked God for Bruce, and then taken credit for having had such excellent judgment in men for one so young. Who he was then is who he is still, a quarter of a century later. He is optimistic, positive, hopeful, and trusting that God's will should be done. Though our lives had become complex, Bruce still operated with that same idealism for making a difference in the world. His faith is simple, like a child's. I am the one who makes faith, and life, and adoption so complicated.

I had always hoped and prayed that Bruce would receive vivid affirmations from God as I had experienced, so there would be no doubts. But maybe *he* didn't *need* confirmation. Bruce's reluctance to adopt always grew out of his concern for his family. My reservations were always about *me* and *my* comforts. This dear man was happy about the adoption, about being Roma's father. Maybe he was fulfilling a youthful desire to change the world, at least his little corner of the world.

I was ashamed that I had pouted at length about the inconveniences imposed on my life, when there was a child who needed what was so easy for me to give, and what wasn't even mine to hoard: love.

Wedding Day, 1978

Chapter Twenty

*"I know the power obedience has of making
things easy which seem impossible."*

Saint Teresa of Avila

Friday morning was bright and beautiful. My heart was filled to overflowing. Bruce was only one of several reasons I had to be thankful. There was my new son, who everyone agreed was quite charming, and my incredibly charitable children at home who I could hug in five days. We were heading into the final leg of our journey.

We all packed up and were off to the airport to fly back to Moscow. Geraldine and Tom were ecstatic to have David with them instead of having to visit him daily at the orphanage. Their joy was complete. I was thrilled to have at last embraced the mission that Bruce and I had been gifted.

Back in Moscow, we parted ways with Geraldine, Tom, and David for the evening. Both families had embassy requirements to obtain: a passport, visa, and a physical exam to be completed for our children before we were allowed to take them home.

Geraldine, Tom, and David went to a hotel. Bruce, Roma, and I were staying with another host family in a Moscow apartment.

We arranged to join them the next day as we would again share our original driver and translator.

We were delivered to a massive complex of identical apartments, probably built in the 1950s. Our aids saw us to the heavy, secure door of our new host. She was a jolly woman, maybe in her late fifties who spoke only a smattering of English. Her daughter would be home in the evening, and she was studying English in high school.

Rina was a sturdy Russian woman, a no-nonsense, practical, yet cheerful, matriarch who had seen much change in her motherland during her lifetime. She fulfilled my stereotype of the typical Russian babushka, unlike the tall, beautiful, stylish women we passed on the street in downtown Moscow. She was generous and loving. I could have taken her home, taught her a little English and let her be another grandmother to me, as well as to Roma. She wasn't old enough to be my mother, but she was a perfect doting grandmother.

Rina was amazing with Roma. They laughed and talked as if he had known her his entire seven and a half years. He still tried to ignore us, but Rina would have none of it! She was stern but pleasant, and he smiled as she had him serve our meals and help her clean up afterwards. She got out her well-worn Russian-English dictionary often to ask us questions or to make suggestions. She recommended that we rest while she took Roma down to the park. We chose to tag along.

The primitive playground consisted of some metal swings, a teeter-totter and a sliding board, all on a hard dirt surface. It was about 5 p.m., and getting quite chilly, but everyone was soon out in the park. Families came. Old ladies in matronly dresses and woolen hats sat and talked. This was clearly a social time. The scene reminded me of my childhood—the same kind of playground equipment and the slower pace of life.

Being a stranger in what I had always thought was a hostile country was truly humbling. I grew up fearing the Soviets, though they were always the disdained "Russians" to my mother's generation. When we played war as children, the Russians were always the enemy. Now, living among this kind, gentle, generous people, I was saddened that they had endured such hardships at the hands of self-serving dictators, and ashamed that we westerners detested the nation as a whole without actually knowing the people or the culture. These average citizens, neighbors visiting in the local park with their kids, didn't like the communists any more than Americans did, but while we were safely separated by a half a globe, they lived shoulder to shoulder with the military presence that, in U.S. estimations, threatened the world.

Rina's daughter, Kate, was a lovely sixteen-year-old. She had been a tiny, sickly six-year-old when Rina first heard about her. It was reassuring to see such a successful love story involving adoption. As a single working woman of moderate means, Rina had sacrificed a lot to adopt. Because Kate had been unwanted by everyone else, Rina had been awarded the small, weak child.

When Rina looked at Kate, I was encouraged that a mother's love was not restricted to biological birth. And Kate adored her mother.

Kate's English was quite understandable, though she was embarrassed by her perceived deficit, and apologized often for not understanding me. My southern accent might have been the culprit.

Roma adored the young beauty. Kate and Rina had many conversations with him that we were not privy to. The three of them laughed like old friends. I got to know Roma better by watching him interact with these two. He was respectful, comfortable, and funny. Occasionally Kate would translate the conversation for Bruce and me when she thought it was worth the time and struggle of coming up with equivalent words.

"Fly away; I will meet you later," was one such conversation Roma had with his helium balloon as he let it escape.

"He's an imp. Do you know that word?" I asked, speaking slowly, so full of pride in the boy with whom God blessed me.

Kate looked pensive and apologetically shook her head. She

grabbed her mother's Russian-English dictionary, and I looked it up for her. She laughed when she read Roma's description. "Oh yes!" she said emphatically. She translated for Rina, and they both laughed, shaking their heads. They were extremely fond of my little boy. He was quite charismatic. Rina watched him proudly, like a grandmother, and repeated the few English words she knew, "Very good boy."

On Sunday, with the embassy and other state buildings closed, we drove around to see the sights of Moscow. We rode by the impressive and prestigious University of Moscow. Our Moscow translator, Katherine, had our driver stop at the Cathedral of Christ the Savior, the largest church in Russia. The original nineteenth-century cathedral had been commissioned by Alexander I in 1812, to give thanks to God for liberating the Russian people from Napoleon. The five gilded domes, of which the central one was the highest, could be seen from any part of Moscow when it was finally completed in 1883.

According to Katherine, the church was demolished in 1931 under the order of Soviet leader Joseph Stalin. On the site of the razed church, ill-fated construction was planned for the Palace of the Soviets. World War II broke out, and plans for the ostentatious tower were abandoned. By 1960, the enormous pit that had been excavated for the foundation had been turned into a swimming pool. It was a common joke among the Russian Orthodox Muscovites that the people who enjoyed the swimming pool on that holy ground for those thirty-some years, were inadvertently being baptized!

As soon as Communism fell in 1991, talk began of rebuilding the cathedral. The construction began in 1995, and the cathedral was blessed in 2000. Our translator proudly explained to us that, though the communists had destroyed their cathedral, the people had rebuilt it. Many citizens had donated their own money in massive amounts, even by American standards, to help restore their place of worship, at a staggering cost of $500 million. To critics, it was an outrage for a country to spend so much when it couldn't pay its wages on time. To supporters, it symbolized the religious resurrection of Russia after seventy years of Soviet oppression.

I grew up believing Russians were atheists. I wondered if, with all our affluence in America, we would have chosen to spend a vast fortune to rebuild a church, replete with golden holy icons, that a political enemy had razed and in its place built a swimming pool! I am afraid we might have been content to let the swimming pool remain.

Next, we drove to a giant black iron structure rising abruptly out of the river, a recent sculpture honoring Peter the Great. It was an excessively tall ship that ascended straight out of the water, metal waves and smaller ships jutting from all directions beneath the massive naval clipper ship. It was an engineering feat: so tall, yet so narrow at the base, it seemed an accomplishment just remaining erect. As an artist and sculptor, I thought it was fascinating, though not beautiful. Our escorts thought it was hideous. There was obviously a controversy surrounding the modern monstrosity among Muscovites.

The markets were fun. They were like flea markets anywhere, with buyers and sellers haggling over treasures. Most of the venders spoke excellent English. I wanted traditional Russian items: mother-of-pearl inlay boxes with hand painted Pushkin fairy tale themes, intricately decorated matryoska (nesting) dolls, carved bear toys, things that would one day remind Roma of his heritage.

I enjoyed the shopping and sightseeing, but our biggest treat came Sunday night. We went to the Moscow Circus with Rina and Kate. Roma reluctantly sat beside me because Rina insisted. She was undoubtedly the boss while we were her guests. I was thrilled to have her in charge. Roma would learn to listen to us, to trust us, later. But for now Rina, had everything under control. The circus was astounding. Roma sat spellbound for two hours!

If I had not been aching to see Taylor, Kellie and Heather, I might have accepted Rina's invitation to extend our stay and see more sights. She talked of the places she longed to show us. She was visibly proud of her home.

Moscow was a beautiful city filled with mystique and contrast. Again I thought of Churchill's summation: "a riddle wrapped in a mystery inside an enigma." Yes, that was Russia. I was trapped in a time warp. The old and the new clashed here. Glitzy storefronts squeezed in alongside gilded, onion-top architecture. Moscow University appeared on the horizon like the city of Oz, promising a brighter future for her citizens, many of whom were struggling at this point in the long, turbulent history of Russia. Red Square's ghosts echoed an era of revolutions and military power, but even in the eerie silence of the district, the specters of hope endured.

The starkness of Lenin's Mausoleum and beyond, the colors of Saint Basil's magnificent cathedral drove home the contrast of the country that is Roma's homeland. We will teach him to be proud of his heritage. The Russian people we had the pleasure of meeting were proud, generous people. They loved their homeland and were protective of the spirit of "Mother Russia," now that she had been liberated, once again.

On Monday morning our driver came to fetch us for the last time. Rina was sad to see us go; she tried a final time to persuade us to stay another night with her and Kate, instead of returning to an Americanized hotel. It was so tempting; she made us feel so welcomed and comfortable. But our arrangements had been made, and it was time for us to spend some quiet time, just the three of us, before it became the six of us back home.

In the two days we had lived with this small family, we had grown to love them. They invited Heather and Kellie, who would have so much in common with Kate, to come to Moscow and stay with them. We invited them to come to America and stay with us. It is remarkable how close you can get to a family, even though you have to struggle to communicate, when you share the common priority of loving children.

Bruce and Roma in front of St. Basil's Cathedral, Moscow

We spent Monday at the American Embassy and other official buildings assuring the legality of our adoption and gaining permission to transport Roma to America. In waiting rooms at the different check points, we saw the same families who were at the same stages of their adoption process.

Roma, like all adoptees, was required to have a physical exam. As the gentle Russian doctor who spoke excellent English examined Roma, he said, "I can see you are going to have trouble."

I held my breath. What can the doctor see that I cannot? Here is the disaster I'd been braced for.

"With the girls," he smiled, sensing my fear. "He has a beautiful smile."

"Yes he does," I agreed.

When all our mandatory tasks were complete, we were delivered to the Marriott Grand, a posh hotel with all the American amenities. We would spend two nights there, so we settled in to enjoy ourselves. Without friends to converse with in Russian, Roma was quiet. He soon started to hold Bruce's hand. His small gesture of trust touched me. I felt I was witnessing the birth of a bond that would last a lifetime. It reminded me of when I had watched Bruce hold our babies for the first time. Roma still didn't have much to do with me, but I had time to be patient. He was cautious. I thought he was a smart boy for taking his time.

We took him to Red Square for the first and perhaps last time of his life. He may go back to Russia one day. I have no idea what God has in mind for this child. We took lots of pictures with pieces of Russian history in the background, just in case.

The Marriott had a beautiful indoor pool. Luckily we had read the travel information and had packed swim suits, and a new one for Roma. Bruce and Roma swam while I operated the video camera. Roma had no fear. He dove into the water, with perfect form, and sank like a rock. He didn't know how to swim. But he clung to Bruce and enjoyed the water. I pleaded with Bruce to stay within grabbing distance as Roma thrashed frantically around in the water to stay afloat. Within the hour, he could swim, however ungracefully, from side to side. And Bruce was his new best friend.

Tuesday, our last full day in Russia, we would indulge in last minute shopping and final sightseeing. With the translator again, Roma excitedly told her about the blue water. He had apparently never seen a swimming pool before. We ate lunch at McDonald's. Somehow, Roma was familiar with McDonald's, though all he would eat were french fries. A coke, apparently his first, burned his mouth.

When we were delivered back to the Marriott Grand, we would not see our driver and translator again. We were on our own. The hotel was providing transportation to the airport the following morning. This was starting to feel official—we had a new son. We walked a few blocks and ordered pizza for dinner. Roma didn't know what it was. As though playing charades, he pretended to break an egg, complete with the little "tick, tick, tick" of taping it to break it, then his little hands opened the imaginary egg, and finally he made a sizzling sound effect. He was asking if the pizza was a giant fried egg. We shook our heads and tried to coax him to taste it, but he was not eager to find out about this American staple. So we stopped again where we knew he would eat, at McDonald's. That night we stayed in our room and packed, while Roma watched American cartoons on TV, gut-laughing at *Tom and Jerry*, a universal cartoon with no words.

While packing Roma's bag, Bruce pulled out two plastic guns, a camouflage machine gun and a pistol.

"We can't take these. What if they stop us?"

True, Americans had gotten a little wacky about toy lookalike weapons, but we were not in America. I was willing to risk it.

"Bruce, they are plastic. Let 'em stop us. We are taking his guns. They are the only toys he has."

Roma's passport

A shiny black Mercedes was prompt Wednesday morning to take us to the airport. After all we had experienced during the past nine days, this show of wealth seemed ironic. We were told to arrive three hours early to the airport to go through the tedious immigration process. The sea of people included many of the families with the small children we had seen at various adoption stations. The immigration booths were serviced by only a few attendants. When we finally stood at the window to show our papers, the woman called Roma by name so she could compare the boy's face to the picture on his passport. "Nyet," he corrected her, "Arthur." I had almost forgotten his choice of his new American name. She looked from the picture to the boy a few times, then waved us through as I held my breath, thankful we had barely dodged an international kidnapping incident!

On the plane going home were many of the same families we passed in the embassy. The plane was like a flying nursery. There must have been fifteen or twenty children and babies on the flight, including some parents with sibling groups. Roma appeared to be the oldest. He made friends with many of the children and adults. Roma knew how to work a room, even if that room was 30,000 feet above the ground. I was so proud of his self-confidence and his warm friendliness. He was a poster child for adoption. His sparkle invited love. An older Russian woman studied him before asking if we knew his nationality. Russian and Georgian was what we had been told.

"Ah, yes," she spoke with that musical Russian accent. "Georgian men are known for being handsome."

Roma was friendly with everyone on the plane. He was as comfortable with adults as he was with children, with English speaking parents as well as with their newly acquired, Russian-speaking children. He moved around the plane and talked to the crying children, soothing them with his fearlessness. He comforted frightened parents as well in the process, injecting them with hope. Everyone, children and parents alike, had fallen in love with our boy.

The next test would be a crucial one. Bruce's parents, Mike and Betty, were picking us up at the airport in Washington. First impressions are the most lasting. When we landed in New York, it was 2 a.m., Roma's time. He had been awake for almost twenty hours, and he was wired. We were about forty-five minutes behind schedule, and the flight attendants had warned us that due to the lengthy wait in immigrations, we might miss our flight to Dulles. I was determined that we were going to be on that flight when it left New York if I had to chase the plane down the runway.

We hurried from the plane and ran to get in the long lines of immigrations. The endless lines did not seem to move. Soon after we got in line, they opened a new booth to expedite the process. They directed us to be the first in the new line. From that point, everything sped along, and we actually had time to sit and rest before we were called for boarding. I even called my sister on her toll-free number from the pay phone to let her know we were back in the country, safe, and close to home.

When we boarded the plane for Dulles, Roma was beginning to crash. The plane was almost empty, and we got to sit by a couple that Roma had flirted with during his many trips to the bathroom. They were returning from Russia after making their first of two mandatory visits to meet their two new children. They would be returning to Russia in three weeks to adopt. They were hungry for hope and for a happy ending. Roma had provided what they needed. They had so many questions, and I felt like we were the voice of experience for them. We talked on excitedly in a language that Roma could not decipher, droning, hypnotizing the exhausted boy until his weary head drooped against the window. He slept an hour. As soon as the plane began the descent, he popped up, rejuvenated.

I was suddenly nervous again about Mike's reaction to meeting Roma. Mike was trying to be supportive, as evidenced by the fact that they had insisted on driving us to the airport and picking us up. But I knew it was difficult for him. What if Roma was tired and cranky from such a long day with so little sleep? *I* was. Maybe he would suddenly be homesick. And confused. He must have questions we could not answer for him.

My in-laws didn't live far from the airport, and soon their car pulled into the far end of the parking lot. We could watch it slowly make its way to us in all the traffic. As we waited, my anxieties grew. When they stopped in front of us, Betty hopped out, hugged us, and took a picture of Roma. She was nervously happy, perhaps experiencing the same fear I had. Roma got in as Mike turned to say an enthusiastic "Hi." Roma held out his little hand for Mike to shake, unprompted. Touched, Mike shook it. Roma soon was enthralled with the big Cadillac, with all its buttons and knobs.

I finally exhaled, knowing everything would be okay. Thank you God! It could not have gone more perfectly. Roma's little extended hand was hard to reject.

We had about an hour drive home to my other babies. I ached to see them.

We drove up to bright and bouncing balloons on the porch railing. Kellie and Taylor ran out of the house as soon as they heard the car. We hugged and then they were off chasing Roma down the street as he squealed gleefully. Soon neighbors stopped by to join the fun. My joy was beyond what I could have imagined. Heather called from college. With such an outpouring of support and love, Mike and Betty had to believe we could do this. And I was beginning to believe it too!

The waterfall that I had dreaded for so long, that had looked and sounded and felt more ominous than Niagara Falls, that had scared the joy out of me, actually provided an amazingly awesome ride, with a surprisingly gentle landing.

Chapter Twenty-One

"My cup runneth over."

Psalm 23:5 (KJV)

We arrived home on Wednesday, the first of May. On Thursday, life returned to relative normalcy for Bruce, Kellie, and Taylor who escaped to work and school. I was abandoned at home with a busy boy. He had me out in the crisp morning as soon as the older two left for school playing badminton in the driveway. Then we traveled to Frederick to the "English Speakers of the Other Languages" (ESOL) office to register him for their services when he started to school on Monday. Roma sat quietly, studiously absorbed by the supplied toys while the coordinator helped me complete paperwork. I hardly recognized the quiet, pensive child who played with plastic trucks, whispering, expressive sound effects for an hour and a half.

"He's so good, so quiet! They are usually bouncing off the walls when they come in here," the coordinator observed.

I simply nodded, hiding my own surprise. I was growing more optimistic about the behavior and abilities of this boy who, though I had known him for such a short time, I would never describe as "quiet."

"We'll try him in second grade," she concluded.

I had expected him to be placed in first grade, maybe even

kindergarten. He would not be eight until August, young for most American second-grade boys. I didn't know much about his previous education. I had not been able to ask questions of his teachers or principal as I had hoped. His initial referral from his orphanage had warned that he was "lazy with his tutors." According to the translators who observed him reading every sign he passed, Roma was a capable reader, but then he was reading Russian. How easy would it be for him to learn English? And any "deficiencies" he had in his early education would be compounded by the fact that the child did not know a word of English, so how could we explain anything to him!

Regardless, I was pleased that he would be in the second grade, partly because, I would tease later, he would be eligible for military school earlier. He was such a little soldier—all of his games were war games, even when playing with dinosaurs. But all kidding aside, I knew this was a bright child who might be bored with younger children. He always gravitated toward older kids and adults. He needed to be challenged. He would quickly catch up academically, once he learned the language, I convinced myself. The ESOL coordinator sensed this worldliness about Roma too.

Friday morning, we stopped by his new elementary school to register him to begin the following Monday, May 6. We met with Mr. Cuppit, the assistant principal. He showed no anxiety about having a new Russian kid at his school. He gave us a tour through the gym, the cafeteria, the library, and finally, the alluring computer lab. "Computer" was the same in both languages, and Roma knew about computers! Mr. Cuppit let Roma play a few minutes on one of the reading programs. It was difficult because of the language barrier, but Roma was very eager to learn. When we left, we drove slowly past the colorful, extensive playground equipment. To Roma it must have looked like Disney Land.

Next stop—the library. It was alive with youngsters. I walked to the children's section expecting Roma to follow me. I turned to see him disappear out the door. He was crossing the parking lot to wait in the car.

He was buckling his seat belt as I got there.

"Roma, books, read," I said stupidly, to no one who could understand.

How could I explain that we were just going to get fun books written in a language that he couldn't comprehend?

"Nyet." He was immovable.

It occurred to me that to Roma the library might resemble another orphanage with many small children and a few caregivers.

We went on to our next destination. Roma liked the grocery store much better. His eyes lit up when he saw so many items he wanted to put in the cart.

"Cheeps!"

They must have had potato chips in Russia! Why we were not filling our cart with a variety of chips and snack items and boxes of cereal in rainbow colors was impossible to explain. But I was determined that I was going to start out strict and not spoil him. I didn't want to have to break any more bad habits later. While we were in Russia, I had bitten my tongue as our charitable hosts had given Roma everything he asked for with that cunning little smile of his. They had given him coffee to drink, shoveling in three or four scoops of sugar. They had allowed him to watch hours of cartoons. I am not a permissive mom, and I knew those habits would be painful to break once I was the enforcer.

I passed on any cereal of unnatural hue and held up one finger to indicate that he could choose *one* bag of chips. He studied, compared, and chose carefully. I liked that in a kid, especially mine!

"Cheeps" he said as soon as we unpacked the groceries at home. I poured some into a bowl and offered them to him. He wanted me to take the bowl; he wanted the bag! After he was sure of my intentions, he left the room and started to cry. His manipulation must have been successful before, but not here. I dumped the chips back into the bag as he watched hopefully from the door. I rolled the top down, put a clip on them, and put them away on a high cabinet shelf. When Roma saw this, the wailing started in earnest. I put the rest of the groceries away and ignored him.

"Cheeeeeps," he cried as he displayed the most pitiful face I could imagine.

"Pishalsta" ("please") he pleaded with hands pursed in prayer formation.

"Nyet," I answered calmly without looking at him.

He cried for five minutes. I was impressed with his fortitude and determination. This behavior had obviously worked for him in the past. I am sure that these traits could be attributes one day, but I was not going to start allowing that behavior for the reward of "cheeps." He was soon distracted and played quietly by himself with little cars.

Later I fixed him a sandwich, with some chips in a bowl, and he ate happily.

On Sunday we went to church. We all attended our respective Sunday school classes. I felt some guilt for depositing this new citizen with an unsuspecting teacher in a class of seven-year-olds. How much damage could he actually do in one hour?

Our class welcomed us back with open arms. We spent the class relating our experiences. As we babbled on, one friend rolled in a shiny, new, black and red bike with training wheels, a gift from our class. We wanted to get Roma immediately, but decided to postpone the bedlam.

With five minutes left of class, we got Kellie and Taylor from their classes, and then retrieved Roma. His eyes lit up when he saw the bike, having no doubts whose gift it was. He hopped on the bike and the other two were off in pursuit, barring stairways, doors leading to the parking lot, and to the sanctuary where the last service of the morning was ending.

Once at home, we parked the tiny bike in the driveway to marvel at its beauty. We might as well have handed him keys. He had wheels! Luckily our street was about one-third of a mile long, had no intersections and ended in a court just past our house. Not many cars or strangers intruded in our neighborhood, so we felt he would be safe wobbling down the street. He protested when he saw the helmet, but we insisted. Roma thought he knew best. Just as he turned to dropkick his helmet into the yard, I lifted the small bike with one hand and locked it in the shed. He turned from his triumphant kick just as I was closing the door on his brand new convertible! He ran to the shed, screeching. We waited it out in the house. Again, he cried longer and louder than I thought humanly possible. I would have to explain to the neighbors later!

An hour later he came with his helmet in hand, a dopey grin on his impish face. He wanted to ride that bike.

He was a fast learner.

Bruce was obviously touched by the little boy who looked up at him and called him "Papa." Bruce encouraged the title. But with the other kids in our home calling him "Dad," it didn't take long for Roma to call him "Dad" too. Bruce would pat his chest and say, "Come to Papa." Roma would laugh and shake his head, and correct him, "Dad." Roma was eager to be in all ways American!

On Roma's first day of school, Bruce took a day off from work, and I returned to the high school to see my other kids. I was eager for my normal routine, if there would ever be "normal" in my life again. Just being back at school gave me indescribable joy. I had missed two weeks of the student's adolescent lives, but it seemed like much longer. The world had continued to turn while we had been on its other side. College decisions had been made; games had been lost; new love had flourished; friends had hurt friends. I had a lot of catching up to do.

Sitting in a different teacher's desk every day never made me feel like a nomad, or a nobody. As the kids came through the doors with a cheerful welcome, my heart always soared. There was no glamour in being a substitute teacher, no cause for vanity. It was the lowest rung on the educational ladder, the chopped liver of school staff, yet I *loved* it. It didn't make sense. In this small servant role, God had not called the equipped; he had equipped *me* for this mission that was my perpetual boot camp. Sometimes the students were difficult, at times, disrespectful, and often, exhausting, yet I always wanted to return for another day, confident that there were those who needed me to care. As God worked on my character, He also rewarded me in simple but meaningful ways. Being accepted by teenagers has its own rewards.

I made no announcements about my trip to Russia or my new son, before or after the journey. I usually talked to the students about *their* lives, not mine. Kellie, who was by then a senior, told her friends, but most of the students had no idea what monumental event had transformed my life.

At home, Bruce was experiencing a different kind of day. We had decided to take Roma to school at two o'clock so his first day would be abbreviated. That way he could ride the bus home and get familiar with the last part of his day. Bruce took him to his classroom door, but Roma refused to go inside. Not wanting to disturb the class of curious students, Bruce had a dilemma. For the hour and a half that remained in the day, Bruce sat at the small table with the other second graders to show Roma how unthreatening the class was. Roma sat on the floor in the hall outside the door to show Bruce who was the boss that afternoon. The image of their switched roles tickled me.

At the end of the day, Roma got on the bus while Bruce drove home. Kellie, Taylor, Bruce, and I all met him at the bus stop at the end of the street. He got off the bus without acknowledging us, walking right past us.

"School, nyet!" He held out his little fist and displayed thumbs down.

Uh oh!

I wondered again if maybe he thought the school was another

orphanage. All evening, whenever we mentioned school, he stubbornly repeated, "School, nyet."

The next morning he was still anxious. I ignored his apprehensions and chattered happily about the bus and school, knowing he couldn't understand my words, but he could understand my attitude.

"Nyet" was all I could understand. He emphatically rattled off strings of Russian. He was probably using some of those spicy words that our interpreter had assured us that he knew.

I walked him down to the bus stop, all the way fearing that he would not get on, and there would be an ugly scene of screaming and a battle of strong wills. But as the bus creaked to a stop, he raced to be the first of the three kids in the neighborhood to climb the steps. I was thankful for that competitive spirit of his that made him always want to be first in line! I received no calls from the school that day, though I was expecting them. When Roma got off the bus that afternoon, I exhaled a sigh of relief when I saw him. His face was elated and animated.

"School, Dah! (Yes!)" Then he gave his first full day at Twin Ridge Elementary School a thumbs up! I was smart enough to know that his enthusiasm had nothing to do with learning. There were kids, and that playground, and best of all, that big yellow school bus brought him home at the end of the day—something that did not happen to Roma in Russia!

A week into his relocation, Roma's flood gate crumbled. We had told him no more TV and turned it off. He started crying. The storm that we knew must be brewing in this tiny tempest finally touched down. Unlike his other tantrums and bouts of frustration and attempts at manipulation, this was a sad and lonely howl. He was hysterical and inconsolable. I feared he was homesick. I had been homesick as a child, and I have never, thank God, found its equal among harbingers of misery. In fact, I, too, felt a twinge of homesickness—I was missing the home of my not-so-distant past, the one in which there was little stress and everyone spoke English!

He was a sad boy that night, perhaps realizing, just as I was, that the change in our lives was permanent. As bad as it may have been for him in Mozdok, that life was comfortable and familiar to this little boy. They could speak Russian. He knew how to work the system. Now he found himself living with strangers in a confusing world. I had no way to comfort him, except by soothing sounds of words he did not understand. He cried himself to sleep as I patted his back. The next day he was okay.

For about two months, periodically he would have grieving sessions, but to lesser degrees each time.

The experts in adoption, the adoptive parents that I had met, had warned that I might experience an adjustment period of sadness, maybe even regret that might last as long as six months. But regret was never part of my adjustment, once Roma had joined our family. I had grieved enough over the decision before he came, I must have gotten it out of my system. I was confident that God had arranged this match; I could hardly second-guess God anymore. Whenever dark moods clouded my perspective, and they did, I knew they would pass. Since our return home, I had no more doubts, no more questions. I knew we had done the right thing by adopting Roma.

Two weeks after we returned, we received a check in the mail for $2,000. It was the State grant that we had applied for, almost too late, that Bruce was certain we would not get because of the poor economic state of Maryland.

The estimated total cost of the adoption before we left for Russia was $22,000. Some of the fees were less than expected. We returned with four hundred dollars, even after our shopping sprees. Total cost: $21,600.

With $5,000 each from the restaurant painting job, the "special needs" adoption grant, and the gift from the Tate's, added to our tax refund of $4,600, and our state adoption grant of $2,000, God had provided $21,600. No funds were borrowed, nor taken from savings to finance Roma's adoption. The Lord not only provided, He was showing off!

Chapter Twenty-Two

"Our love should not be just words and talk; it must be true love, which shows itself in action."

1 John 3:18 (GNT)

Three weeks into Roma's Americanization, I was invited to join his class on a field trip. Actually, I was *required* to attend if Roma was going. His teachers worried about what might happen if he was released into the wild outdoors of a Catoctin Mountains nature hike. Matthew's mother related that her son had come home one day and said he had a new friend at school. It was several days later when Matthew casually mentioned that his new friend, Roma, didn't speak any English. No matter what words are spoken, all children laugh in the same language!

He was picking up new words daily. He was extremely social and was highly motivated to communicate with his new friends. To watch Roma interact with the kids, one wouldn't know he had been in the United States for less than a month.

His ESOL teacher came three mornings a week for an hour each time. At first she would just take him out to the playground to play and get used to her.

The teacher didn't know exactly what to do with him, so she allowed him to play computer games while the other students listened attentively to their lessons. He was picking up words quickly, but his pronunciation made his speech difficult to decipher and frustrating for everyone. The school requested a Russian interpreter to explain school rules and expectations to Roma. I was invited to attend. The translator was a sweet, gentle, and pretty woman. Roma responded well to her.

One of Roma's "problems" at school was hanging his arm over the shoulders of his new buddies. In our culture of respecting others' "personal space" and "keep your hands to yourself" mentality, Roma's warmth was not always appreciated. The interpreter explained the cultural differences to Roma by touching his face and arm gently as she illustrated to the adults present the difference between American and Russian displays of camaraderie. The teacher had requests for Roma concerning classroom rules: he needed to stay in his seat, acknowledge the teacher when she called his name, and not take the other children's food at lunch time. I felt a pang of sympathy for the smiling, oblivious boy. At the orphanage, the food on the table belonged to everyone, so Roma was just helping himself. He didn't understand personal possessions. The interpreter explained the expectation, speaking softly to Roma, and they conversed cheerfully. This must have been comforting to Roma. She would laugh occasionally, genuinely amused with him.

"He is very sweet," she stopped once to report.

His teacher, the assistant principal, the reading specialist, and I sat quietly around the table as these two babbled in Russian, solving the problems of the world, at least of Twin Ridge Elementary School, as they related to one small, energetic Russian seven-year-old.

She finished by translating for the rest of us a dialogue that amused her: after she explained the school policies to Roma, she paused and asked, "Will you start to obey the rules tomorrow?"

"No" was his determined answer, a big, mischievous grin on his face.

She was worried that maybe he was more difficult than she had first thought. "Why not?" she asked.

"Because we do not have school tomorrow!" she translated for us.

It was true; they did not have school that Friday.

Everyone laughed as the boy blushed.

"I can tell he is intelligent because of his advanced sense of humor," Mr. Cuppit said with approval.

Mr. Cuppit was learning what I already knew.

We finished the school year in mid-June with a school-wide picnic. It was fun to see Roma interact with the other kids and teachers. Everyone knew Roma. The sugary voices of the girls made me think back to the doctor's warning in Russia: "You are going to have trouble with the girls."

I tried not to glare at the hopeful, young flirts. They couldn't help themselves.

After lunch, a magician performed in the auditorium. From my seat in the back, I could watch Roma. He was spellbound. When the magician asked for volunteers from the audience, hands waved wildly; Roma's hand shot up too. I prayed that he wouldn't be chosen. He wasn't. I imagined the unsuspecting performer trying to ask questions or give commands to a boy who knew approximately twenty words of English! Roma didn't know his language issue was a barrier; he just wanted to be a part of the magic; he just wanted to be like the other kids. His kidness, his curiosity, and spontaneity overshadowed any language obstacle. Roma was not shy and introverted; he was determined to squeeze as much fun as possible out of every opportunity that presented itself.

Here is a partial list of words Roma knew by the time school ended in mid-June, though many were not understandable without visual aids: remote control, Gamecube, "cheeps," scooter, bike, TV, thank you, yes, excuse me, computer, school, and bus. I soon recognized his versions of expressions I used too often like "thankyousomuch" and "oh-mah-doh-mahs"("Oh my goodness," I think), each pronounced as one word.

Taylor was worried when he heard him say the latter.

"I think they are teaching him bad things on the bus. It sounds like he's saying 'I'm a dumb ass.'" Taylor looked sheepish as he said the forbidden words, but he clearly thought his mom should know. I repeated Roma's new expression aloud. "Oh-mah-doh-mahs." It did sound like "I'm a dumb ass." I assured Taylor, though not so sure myself, that he was simply repeating my overused expression. I carefully enunciated my "Oh . . . my . . . goodness" after that, and soon Roma's version was clearly not profanity. He was like a parrot.

"Not my fault" he responded to my complaints one evening. I laughed knowing he must have heard this before. Nothing was anyone's fault at my house.

After three months in America, he began talking clearly. His pronunciation was much better, especially after he had seen the word spelled. He left out connective words and often had the wrong verb tense, but we had no problem communicating with him.

Kellie played board and card games with him all summer. He did not like to lose. When he did lose, he would cry. At these times, we would stop playing and put the game away. Roma didn't understand why we wouldn't give him a break. It was as if he was saying, "Hey, I'm just a poor orphan from Russia, why won't you let me win?" He, like most children, was willing to use whatever advantage he had.

We enjoyed playing with him because he was competitive. He liked the game *Sorry!*. It was the first game he mastered. In the game, the players take turns drawing cards and moving around the board to get all four pieces "home" first. Not all the cards have numbers; some instruct players to move backwards, switch places with opponents, or return to start. Kellie only told him once, and Roma remembered what each card meant, even though I always had to read the card for my turn! What most fascinated us about Roma's *Sorry!* skills was that he didn't count the spaces he would move. If he drew a number twelve, he would simply pick up his piece and set it down on the right square. Kellie and I would be counting each time, but he was always right. Taylor often theorized that Roma was actually a Russian spy with an implanted chip for artificial intelligence. This skill supported Tay's theory.

There have been occasions when Taylor has kicked himself for supporting the adoption. Taylor was expecting what we all were expecting: a shy, damaged little fellow who would need a lot of acceptance and would perhaps follow Taylor around. Taylor was ready to step into the role of a big brother. What God sent us was a confident little dictator trying to take charge at our house. Sometimes Taylor has resented Roma, and then has chided himself for his honest feelings. And he has been jealous. But most of the time, he has been generous, loving, and mature. He gave up more than anyone to share his family with Roma. They fight like real brothers sometimes, but I guess that is what I should hope for.

I listened to Roma play with plastic animals, soldiers, dinosaurs, or even cars. The sound effects were the same: those of war. At first he talked expressively to his toys in Russian. Soon he spoke no words, but his realistic sound effects continued. After about three months, some English words entered into the conversations. While pointing his gun at me, he would say, "Put your hands up, you're under duress."

"You have no idea, little buddy!" I would tease.

During the summer, Roma began to read easy books, almost effortlessly, again backing up Taylor's "implanted intelligence chip" theory. Often he knew how to sound it out but didn't know the meaning of the word. I was astounded. Many Russian letters that look the same have different sounds, like "v" sounds like "w" and vice versa. Roma would pretend he was a "wampire" and suck blood from "weins." In Russian, each letter made a single sound, but in complicated English, each vowel could make many different sounds. Even consonants aren't consistent. I could understand why it would be difficult to learn. But surprisingly, words like "knight" and "cough" and "phone" were only hard the first time. "Crazy English," he would say when I pronounced those rule-breaking words for him. I only had to tell him once what an odd word was, and it was filed away in that computer chip permanently.

"What is meeld wyolence?" he asked in his choppy, accenting-no-syllable English one day. I had no idea. I just kept repeating it, hoping it would strike a familiar chord. When it was clear that I was not going to figure it out, he ran for a visual aid. He brought back a video case and pointed to the rating: "Mild Violence."

At night we would read. I would read one page, and Roma would read the next. He liked books like *The Cat in the Hat* and *Green Eggs and Ham*. His expressive and sing-songy "Thahnk you. Thahnk you, Sahm Ah Ahm" always got to me. I listened carefully to that beautiful husky little Russian accent, lamenting that the accent would fade over time.

When school resumed in August, I knew his educators would be amazed at his progress. About a month after school started in the fall, Roma's third grade teacher "Ms. Smith" (not her real name) requested a conference with me, along with the assistant principal, his ESOL teacher, the media specialist, the reading specialist, and the ESOL coordinator for the county. I attended beaming.

We started our meeting by the assistant principal asking his teacher, Ms. Smith, how much she thought he was getting out of his day at school.

Roma's first school picture, 2002

"Almost nothing" was the surprising answer. It was her belief that Roma benefitted little from his instruction, and without an aide, she was not capable of meeting his needs in a regular classroom. She didn't have time to spend teaching him all he did not know, to go back and teach him kindergarten, first grade, and second grade materials, and there were twenty-some other kids in the class. Her eyes seemed to bulge more with each statement of failure. She believed he was getting nothing out of school. She didn't think he was able to progress while being mainstreamed. Her frustration was apparent. She went on and on, but I was daydreaming, planning my rebuttal. I was wondering who these school employees were going to believe, and I suddenly felt outnumbered. "Ms. Smith" concluded by pleading with me to send Roma to the ESOL program in Frederick. I had looked into that option when he first arrived. He would ride the bus from home to Twin Ridge, where another bus would pick him up and drive him for another thirty minutes to the ESOL School. He would reverse that procedure every afternoon. Two hours each day on a school bus seemed terribly cruel for an active boy!

I had already been convinced that the ESOL school was not a place for a Russian-speaking student— he might come home speaking more Spanish than English, since the ESOL program catered mostly to Spanish-speaking students.

His ESOL aid spoke next. "This has not been my experience at all. I think he understands a lot. I am amazed at his progress in only four months. It's hard to believe that this is the same child who I last saw in June."

I jumped in, tired of being patient. He had learned to read, I told them excitedly. I even brought a few of the recent books he had completed. They seemed doubtful. "Ms. Smith" said Roma had shown them nothing of his ability to read. "Of course he can't read, you idiot. He barely speaks English," I read between the lines of her condescending tone. The reading specialist intervened to clarify that he had a remarkable memory, and probably remembered each book when I read it to him. His "reading along" might cause me to believe he could read. He had even done that in her reading group. She had tested him, and he had shown her no evidence that he knew how to read. I was slow in understanding, but soon I realized that no one around this table believed me. Even his English tutor, who agreed he had made considerable progress, had seen no evidence that he could read.

It occurred to me that Roma was smarter than all of us. The little stinker was smart all right. The telling image drifted into my mind. I could imagine Roma sitting happily in front of a computer screen as the rest of the class attended to mundane class work.

"You know, as long as he is allowed to do nothing but play on the computer, that's all he is going to do. He doesn't want you to know what he is capable of, because then he will have to *do* it. Test him again, and I'll come to observe. He won't try to fool you if I am there," I challenged.

The staff patronizingly agreed. A few days later I met with Mrs. Verdi, the reading specialist and Roma. She opened her resource book to a beginner reader with three or four words per page. Roma read without hesitation. The teacher glanced up at me. I struggled with my smugness.

"Easy or hard?" she asked my little scholar.

"Easy."

She thumbed to a more advanced level, and again Roma read flawlessly. She skipped several levels and again he read.

She glanced at me again.

"Are you surprised?" I asked.

"Very."

She continued to increase the difficulty until Roma slowed down and struggled with the words. I beamed. Roma was visibly proud of himself.

"Well, that is an instructional level. We'll stop at level nine."

I didn't know what "nine" meant, but I knew it was higher than one through eight. About six weeks later Mrs. Verdi called to report she had tested him again, and Roma was at level seventeen! She was enthusiastic. Mrs. Silver, the assistant principal, stopped me in the hall outside her office when I arrived to pick Roma up one day.

"I just wanted to tell you that I have been hearing wonderful things about Roma's progress. He is exactly where he belongs, here, and not at the ESOL school. You were right. You know best—you are his mother."

Yes, I am his mother.

In the meantime, Roma's teacher quit, just like that. Although school officials assured me Roma wasn't responsible, I had my doubts. A new teacher came in as a replacement. Ms. Pryzbocki understood this boy. She shared that when she was hired, she had been warned that she had a Russian boy in her class who did not speak English. But she said as soon as she met Roma, she knew there would be no problems.

God is always looking out for Roma!

Twenty-Three

*"Let your religion be less of a theory
and more of a love affair."*

G. K. Chesterton

I had witnessed the hugs Roma had so generously given the Russian adults when he visited us through the Cherry Orchard week in November 2001, and when we were in Russia. He seemed reluctant to trust us Americans with his affections. Until he had been with us for almost six months, he would not let anyone hug him. He wanted no part of it, especially if adults were trying hard. I didn't try often; I was patient. His refusals were adamant, but playful. He was more affectionate with his school buddies than with his family. I think he was reluctant to treat us like "family."

"No touchy," he would say as arms extended to him. I would shake his hand when he offered it, and later steal kisses from him while he slept like an angel. He said kisses were "scustin." Unexpectedly, one day as we were standing in the kitchen, he put his arm around my waist and gently squeezed. It was unmistakably a hug. I didn't say anything for fear that if I made a big deal about it, it might be my last for a while.

That night after our reading, Roma said, "Today I hug you."

"I know, thank you," I said.

"I hug you again," and he did. Now he hugs all the time—Taylor, Kellie, Heather, Bruce, me, everyone he knows *well* gets a hug. He still uses discretion; people he isn't familiar with still get a firm handshake.

Walking down the aisle at the grocery store, he puts his arm around my waist. "I love you mom" he says, unprompted. If I put his favorite cereal in the cart, he is thankful beyond reason.

"Thahnk you, mom, really much! I so happy."

Me too.

In the fall, a choir from a Russian orphanage came to a local church to sing, to raise money for their orphanage. Like many other families associated with Frank Adoption Center, we attended. They sang like angels and even included a song with English words they had learned for the occasion. Roma was a little anxious to be around Russian-speaking kids again. After the concert, the American children had an opportunity to ask the choir members questions through a translator, but Roma clung to me and did not want to go near the visitors.

Roma watched the Russian Orthodox priest who accompanied the children. He was an unusually tall, slender man dressed in all black. He had a long gray beard and wore a black stovepipe hat.

"He is God?" Roma whispered earnestly. His innocence and trusting nature endeared him to me in quantum leaps.

We discovered Roma's friend Yevgeniy was adopted by a family in West Virginia with five biological children. His sad eyes had often come to mind since the day we last saw him at the Vladikavkaz Children's Home. I had often wondered if I was supposed to adopt him too. I always inquired about him whenever I spoke to anyone at Frank Adoption Center. I was thrilled when I heard he had a new home.

We got to see him with his new family at a Frank Adoption Center reunion in Alexandria, Virginia, in November 2002. Also in attendance were Dima, the translator from Roma's Cherry Orchard Program, and Tanya, his region's coordinator who we had last seen in Moscow. Roma ran to hug them. He proudly wore his new red, white, and blue "USA" shirt, pointing it out to each one in turn. Roma showed off his English vocabulary, and refused to converse with the others in Russian. Yevgeniy, who had chosen "Jacob" to be his new American name, knew little English, so the young friends laughed and gestured to each other. Roma patted Jacob's hump on his back, just checking to see if it was still there. His mother reported his surgery was scheduled, and the doctors expected favorable results in correcting his severe scoliosis. Roma had grown taller than Jacob. The slender boy's bones looked sharp under his new shirt, but young Jacob's smile was radiant, full of pride, love, and belonging. Seeing him was another glorious gift, in a year of bountiful rewards.

His new mom was eager to meet Roma. She had heard much about him. It turned out that when they had traveled to Vladikavkaz, they too stayed with Svetlana and Solz, and Elena had been their translator. Jeane, Jacob's mom, told how popular Roma had been with his hosts. They had shared many funny stories about Jacob's little buddy Roma.

For Halloween, Roma transformed into a Power Ranger. He wanted to stop between houses and eat the newly added candy. He asked if he could go Trick or Treating again the next night. I had to explain Halloween was only a once-a-year event, that people didn't keep candy on hand to give out every night. But I did allow him to sleep in his costume for several nights. I didn't mind getting my money's worth!

It was fun for all of us to have a little one again at Christmas, with all the magic and mayhem. I feared for the safety of our nine-and-a-half-foot tree. It stayed erect, despite Roma's exuberance, because we tied it to nail in the wall. Roma was thankful for every present he opened. Bruce's parents and grandmother came and stayed a couple of nights. They enjoyed his excitement. The enthusiasm I knew they would feel for this boy had grown since the moment they had first seen him. They treated him like a real grandson. We never spoke of their early trepidation.

Snow began falling the afternoon of Christmas Eve and continued into the evening on Christmas Day. All the winter gear Roma would need, boots, snow pants, gloves, I had bought and wrapped up so he would have sensible presents to open. I tried to go easy on toys. He would remember his first Christmas for years to come. I didn't want that memory to be a barrage of toys.

"Why Santa 'Clous' not go to Russia?" Roma asked after the holidays.

This was a painful question for me to attempt to answer.

"Did you celebrate Christmas in Russia, Roma?"

"We ate leetle cakes." He stared off, and I knew he was remembering. "Maybe I know why Santa not come. Maybe we bad."

My anger flared, but not at him, and somehow he knew it. My rage was with the injustice of a world that looked away and let children suffer. I had looked away and refused to see. Now I saw. I saw pampered, spoiled Americans with all our excess and a fat Santa offering unneeded, unwanted, and often unappreciated gifts as orphanages and probably many families as well, celebrated the birth of Jesus with "leetle" cakes. The contrast made me ache with shame. Our example of Christmas had caused others in the world to feel that they had failed, that they were not worthy. I was beginning to see that we were the ones who had failed.

"Roma, you weren't bad. None of you were bad."

"One nice teacher gave me leetle toy once," he added, watching me, almost in an effort to ease my grief.

For once I was looking forward to the day when the "magic" of Christmas and the true identity of Santa Claus could be exposed to a child of mine. Then he would understand why the children of Russia were passed over by an unknowing, unseeing, and uncaring Santa. I was tempted to drop to the floor beside him and explain the whole farce, but he had been so excited by our neighbor who had come to pay him a visit a few days before Christmas, dressed in full Santa regalia, bearing a gift for the new boy from Russia in our neighborhood.

"None of you were bad," I repeated. "There are just so many children."

It wasn't a convincing response. But it was all I had the energy for.

The winter was particularly snowy with sometimes four feet of snow on the ground at one time. Roma was not fond of the cold stuff. He would play with Taylor and the neighborhood children when it just covered the ground, but he feared being lost in the deep drifts of the white powder. He was suddenly afraid of being misplaced by his new family. He had grown rather attached to us.

He loved to cuddle at night. During our snuggling sessions, he revealed more of his pre-America life story, now that we could understand his English. Snippets usually came in the dark: His family lived in a crowded city with tall buildings, at least by comparison—we lived in a comfortable home, in a rural suburb. According to Roma's recollections, Mozdok was cold, but it didn't snow often. At least he didn't remember snow, but maybe he didn't get to play outside. His grandmother lived with his family, but like his parents, she drank often, and was unkind to him. She found little humor in having the small boy dump the family's alcohol supply down the kitchen drain. The backlash from this innocent but profound effort to correct the problems in his family seriously hampered any pleasant memories of his grandmother. There was another grandmother who lived not too far away where he would go when he ran away from home. I tried not to wince as I imagined the five year old, or younger, sneaking out of a drunken household and running to the safety of his grandmother, a grandmother of whom I had not been aware before, for whom now I had compassion. She must be aching for this lost grandson because a child of hers had neglected the duties of parenthood. This grandmother had no rights, no control over the welfare of her grandchildren. She was nice—I could feel it when he spoke of her. She sometimes allowed him spend the night at her house. He related his stories without emotion, rather matter-of-factly, as if he were recalling someone else's childhood.

When patches of grass finally appeared again, Roma was eager to abandon hibernation. He played, for the first time, on a soccer team, and though his English was not perfect, he loved this game. He did not, however, always understand his coach's shouted directions.

"Get back in the wing, Roma!" The coach seemed to know Roma's name better than any other player! And it never seemed that Roma knew exactly what a "wing" was. But it was a joy to watch his enthusiasm, his coordination, his athleticism, and his joy. I had never been a soccer mom before!

Twenty-Four

*"The reward for obedience and love is
that He will show Himself to you."*

Henry Blackaby, *Experiencing God*

Taylor says it best: he can't think of Roma as a "brother" yet, so he considers him an "exchange student from God." Leave it to Taylor to put it in the proper perspective! Maybe that's how we should all think of our children.

Roma's English is not perfect, but his Russian is gone. I had hoped that he would maintain his birth language. We had lined up someone who spoke Russian who agreed to meet periodically with Roma. But Roma hid behind us at the first attempt, refusing any discourse in Russian. He had wanted to embrace his new country and language and to put his old life behind him. Although I knew that he might one day regret losing his native tongue, I hadn't wanted to confuse him. I had wanted him to feel completely one of us. The price was his ability to speak Russian. Except for his broken English and that adorable thick accent, one would never know that he was one of those cast-off children that I was afraid to love.

In Russia, his country had not let him down. His guardians had cared for him and taught him manners and shown him compassion and love. They had allowed him to trust. They had not broken the spirit of this strong-willed little despot. They had mothered him and so many other forsaken children and ultimately did the only thing they could do, they let them go. By the thousands, the children of Russia are migrating to new homes in foreign lands. I remember what the judge had said at our court hearing: This was their national tragedy, losing their children, but they had to do what was best for the little ones.

The adjustment of adopting an older child has been nothing as I had feared. Instead of trouble and strife, there has been so much joy—joy about Roma and about God's presence in our lives. Joy for our family and for the people around us who have been touched. The laughter that rolls so effortlessly out of this funny little boy supplies us with tremendous delight; his love provides bountiful pride; and the strong energy of his mere presence rewards us with the honor of being part of his life.

"You wanna pizza me?" he asks, little fists in fighting formation, his belligerence belied by his devilish grin. He entertains everyone and is comfortable, unlike my other reserved, sophisticated children, with being the center of attention. He commands that role.

"Yonna play a game?" he asks. We do, but we know he will beat us. He can hold his own against those of us who are many times his age. And his luck is phenomenal, and maddening. I play to win, even against small children, but in Roma, I have met my match!

One weekend Roma and Taylor fished for hours with a new friend. Roma didn't mind holding the pole, but baiting the hook was somebody else's job! He watched with fascination while the experienced friend crammed the hook into the worm. The memory must have lingered because, later that evening, when he was having a snack after dinner, a rectangular apple pastry, he hacked off pieces with his fork and mechanically shoved them into his mouth. After he had eaten over half of it, he said to himself, "It's like a big, fat, nasty worm; I don't know why I'm eating it." And then he shoveled in the last bite.

Being a part of a family again is an adjustment for Roma too. Being the fourth child in an established family, Roma, being competitive by nature, is learning to seize his fair share. He insists on having all eyes on himself. My mother and sister were talking about Taylor's beautiful, dark eyes, trying to give him some much deserved attention. Taylor was obviously enjoying the compliment. Roma would not be left out!

"I have big eyes too," he said. When they didn't answer him, he repeated, a little louder this time, "I have big eyes, too," as he spread his eyes open wide with his thumbs and forefingers.

He always has a fitting comment, an epigram that becomes a slogan for the family. I had a fender-bender while rushing him to soccer practice, late as usual. Roma is the late one, not me. I am compulsively prompt, but Roma is never in a hurry. I was unfamiliar with the area, and by the time I discovered my right hand turn, I was in the left hand lane. I looked briefly, and moved over, right into the car that was hiding in my blind spot. The damage was minimal, but the noise was impressive. After I got out, examined both cars, exchanged insurance information with the other driver and got back in the car, Roma said simply, "Thank you God for we did not die."

After about nine months, when he could communicate well, he began sharing stories about his life in Russia, with no signs of pain. Matter-of-factly he talked about his father hitting him, his mother drinking. "Cute little Rostislav; he's just a baby," he would say, staring off like he could see right before him the baby brother who would be four and a half. Mostly he talked about his sister Liana: finding him food in the streets, visiting him at the Mozdok Children's Home, bringing him candy, and loving him. The part about Liana, who is ten years his senior, always breaks my heart. Between them there was true love, and that loss is tragic. I look at Kellie who is only one month older than Liana. Could Kellie, at seventeen, have signed a legal document relinquishing her legal rights to her younger brothers? One month before her eighteenth birthday, Liana had no legal rights, no choice but to sign. But would she ever forget the two little brothers whom she had taken care of better than their own mother, whom she had visited, and said goodbye to, partly so they might have a better life, but mostly because she had no power to prevent it? The outrage, helplessness, and hopelessness that the young woman must have experienced will forever haunt me. I pray she has peace. I suspect that she knows *this* little brother well enough to know that he will make a way to survive.

This remarkable little boy walked away from everything familiar to him, determined to have a successful life. It was either sink or swim, and Roma is definitely a swimmer.

I shudder to think that I almost turned down the opportunity of being Roma's mom. If I had declined, I would never have known the blessing of loving Roma—of the great gift of being loved by him. I'm sure that if I had ignored this call, I would have suffered in guilt for turning away from God, and I might never have turned back to God. Our life was perfect, I thought, inside our comfortable little box. God pried me out, in the midst of my spoiled tantrums, and opened the door to a mansion I did not know existed.

When people ask, and they always ask, why we decided to adopt, especially an older boy from Russia, with all the potential problems, I pause to think how to answer. I want to gush about the note to a kind student that led to the "adoption" signs, the miracles, and our amazing God, but they don't have time to hear the whole story. I have to be brief and not overly zealous—otherwise, I'll either lose their attention as I ramble on, or perhaps be dismissed as a fanatic. My response always includes that God picked Roma for our family.

As I struggle to answer adequately, I see the skeptics visibly pull away with the mention of God. Nothing I can say will help them understand the miracles that I have lived. I love the draw-nearer, tell-me-more types, whose arm hairs stand on end and tears flood their eyes while I tell them a fraction of the story. Polls consistently report that over eighty percent of Americans profess a belief in God. Why is it easy to say we believe, but difficult to accept that God speaks to us and requires our obedience? The answer is because we are afraid to trust, as I know too well, from having tread those waters.

I remember every day the words of my brilliant eldest son Taylor, "I don't think God is doing this for Roma."

I don't either.

I have heard whispered, "Well done, good and faithful servant," in a thousand little ways, in Roma's 1000-watt smile and his joyful nature, by witnessing my wonderfully patient husband molding Roma's character, and through the quiet nods and affirming smiles from my friends. But the story is not over yet. Every day is a new challenge in the old struggle to lose my stubborn will and depend on God. The devil still puts fear in my heart, and fear is the enemy. But I have seen God in the faces of my friends who believed, in my faithful husband, in my children and their young but exploding faith, and in the many miracles that God has used to orchestrate Roma's adoption and adjustment. Life will never again be accidental, random, or circumstantial. Or Godless. Every feeble attempt I have made at obedience has been rewarded disproportionately in miraculous ways of God revealing Himself to me and to those close to our family.

I remember Henry Blackaby's remarkable book, *Experiencing God*. Who knew I would have my own personal story of experiencing God!

Roma, Heather, Kellie, and Taylor, 2003

April 2003: At the one year anniversary of the adoption of our bundle of energy, magnetism, and joy, I celebrated with thanksgiving. His gestation, labor, and delivery were the most remarkable of my four children—it lasted two years! But the pleasure and pride of having a new "baby" was no less than the other three family additions.

As well as being the mother of Heather, Kellie, Taylor, and now Roma, I still had 1400 other children at Linganore High School. A joyful epiphany settled over me one morning at school while I sat at a desk filling the vacancy of an absent teacher. Earlier in the morning I had heard Patrick, a senior who had been a friend since he was a freshman, call out "Mom" as he so often greeted me. He was Kellie's friend and was at our house often. Suddenly the connection was clear: Roma's adoption was not so different from subbing. I had not wanted to be a substitute teacher. Kellie, with Bruce's help, bamboozled me into it, thankfully. But it was much easier than the next step of adoption, when God did the bamboozling!

I never imagined I could love these students who had started out as strangers intruding on my sheltered and comfortable life. I had sent them to the principal's office. I had written referrals.I had held them accountable for bad choices. I had hugged them when they returned from suspensions. I had swelled with pride over their accomplishments. I had cried over their heart aches. I had unconsciously treated them like my own children, because I had unintentionally fallen in love with them.

I looked back to my first day at the middle school, where I only subbed a half a dozen times. I remembered gentle Anthony whose kindness inspired a note of thanks that set the stage for a startling revelation. Would any high school student have been so kind to a first-time substitute teacher? As much as I love them now, they typically think of ways to abuse the sub, not help the sub. God is incredible. He manipulated every seemingly minor incident to achieve His purpose. He had allowed my vanity so as to mistake the high school students' enthusiasm for a sub, any sub, as fondness for me. That misinterpretation had led me to act more kindheartedly toward the students, and a priceless cycle of affection began. I had often joked that God had given me a supernatural love for teenagers. It was a humbling moment when I realized that God had gone before me in my mission field at the high school and given *them* a supernatural love for *me*!

I have sometimes felt remorse in being so resistant to the call to adopt, and for leaving Roma so long in the Mozdok Home for Children without a family. But God never wastes His time. It had taken Him two years to prepare a terribly stubborn and self-centered mother-to-be for the enormous assignment of being the mom of a stranger. And He used these students of Linganore High School to teach me that I could be a substitute mom!

I look forward to bedtime at our house, partly because I am eager to relinquish this active little soldier, Roman Sudzhashvili Michael, for twelve hours to Snooze City. Bedtime has always been a sweet time in our family. We read our book and talk about things of grave importance, like why dinosaurs are dead, and if a dog can actually play baseball, and if Roma can visit Russia to see Liana for one day, but not spend the night.

After his questions comes Roma's favorite part.

"Tell about Roma," he asks as he snuggles down into his covers, all warm and clean in his new Spiderman pajamas, complete with webbing under the arms. His cracked-marble green eyes shine by the dim nightlight. He knows this story.

"Well…" I try to remember exactly how I started the last time, or he will correct me.

"God said to me one day, 'Debbie, there is a little boy in Russia who I need you to go get. His name is Roma.'"

"And then what?" asks my sleepy boy.

"The devil said 'No!' You don't want to get him. You already have Heather, Kellie, and Taylor. Let someone else take care of Roma."

"And what did God say?" Roma asks because he loves this part.

"God said, 'Yes! You go get him; he is a very special little boy. He is the boy I picked out especially for your family. And he needs you.'"

Roma interrupts, "And what did the devil say?"

"Oh, that bad devil, he said 'No! You really don't want to get Roma. It will ruin your life. Leave him in Russia. He will be okay there. He really doesn't need a mom and a dad, or sisters and a brother to love him. Forget about him.'"

"And what next?" my inquisitive, handsome little thinker asks. He knows what comes next.

As he grows, he will understand on deeper and deeper levels that my bedtime story version is precisely how it happened.

I am so thankful that God had the final word.

The end—and the beginning.

Kellie and Mike's wedding, 2006

Taylor's graduation, 2006

Heather and Rob's wedding, 2009

Kellie and Mike with Abigail, Jack, and Iris, 2011

Rob and Heather with Olive, 2011

Afterword

April 2012: A decade passes quickly. Our family continues to grow, with the addition of two sons-in-law, and four grandchildren. Roma is now seventeen, and as assertive and self-confident as ever. When people congratulate us on doing a good job parenting him, we are quick to confess that this is the boy God sent us. We have just been hanging on for the ride, and it has been a tumultuous journey, "tumultuous" as described by Encarta Dictionary: "Noisy and unrestrained in a way that shows excitement or great happiness." Our journey has been accentuated by noisy excitement alternating with butting heads with a strong-willed child!

I remember Taylor's words: "Maybe after we adopt, other people will see us and want to adopt too," I hope that is true, *if* God is calling them to adopt. But I hope people will read our story and be inspired to surrender to whatever God is calling them to, no matter how threatening the call might appear. I thought I knew better than God what I needed. I was of course wrong. What Got wanted was for me to walk with Him, step by step, not worrying where the steps would lead. In our case, at the end of that trip He blessed us with another son and a quantum leap in our faith!

Have the past ten years been easy? Emphatically NO, but it has been an unrivaled phenomenon which, in many ways, defines who I am.

Concerning his education, what Roma lacks in motivation, he has tried, and often succeeded, to make up for in charm. Schmoozing teachers has been Roma's playful pastime. So, for his junior and senior years, he is preparing for the future at Fork Union Military Academy, an all-boys prep school in Virginia, where, without the distraction of cell phones, tech toys, and girls, Roma should graduate in June 2013.

Roma saw a counselor who specializes in "adoption trauma" to explore any issues that might be buried from an early life of neglect. According to her, older adopted children are difficult to parent. This came as no surprise! She speaks from experience as she adopted two older Russian boys. Using "car" language, she calls them "used" children. I think they simply have "more mileage" on them, perhaps miles down dark roads that we cannot fathom.

Wherever Roma's early side roads took him, one fact has become evident: Roma had people in his early life who truly loved him. His counselor said he was remarkable in the fact that he appears to have no "adoption trauma," and that he has an uncanny ability to take a negative and turn it into a positive. She concluded that someone early on had given him the love he needed. I think I know who.

In my daydreams, (and if I am good at anything, it is daydreaming), I imagine this book being a vehicle of somehow reconnecting Roma with his sister Lianna, now 28, and maybe even Rostilav, his brother, now 12, who would have no memory of Roma. Our family owes Lianna an enormous debt of gratitude. From Roma's stories, a picture of Lianna emerges: She took care of her little brother, visited him in the orphanage with gifts of candy, and she had no choice but to let him go for a better life than she was equipped to provide. She apparently eased him through a difficult childhood, as she, a child herself then, was suffering the loss of her family. He is more of a whole person because of her love and sacrifice. I want her to know that he is loved. He is my son, of whom I am well pleased.

I will end with another true story, a short one this time. Yet unpublished, it is one of many stories that lie dormant in the memory of my computer. This story of a couple of typical days in our life with Roma summarizes the past ten years at our house.

This is My Son

When I heard his bedroom door slam with force, I stomped to my own room and resisted the urge to do the same. I reminded myself that I was the adult.

As usual, I didn't see this skirmish coming. It started benignly, with me reminding my fifteen-year-old of his responsibilities.

As usual, Roma replied absently, "I'll do it later," while watching TV.

"Roma, if I had wanted it done later, I would have asked *later*." I chose my words and tone deliberately, to sound calm, reasonable, and in charge. "You are done with TV for now. When you have straightened up your room, you can go out and help Dad shovel snow."

"*What?*" Roma barked at me, his green eyes bulging with hostility. "There is too much snow to shovel! It is like ten feet deep." Roma's hyperbole is legendary.

"Roma, I am not arguing with you. If you have any hope to watch TV later, you need to do your chores, now."

My early resolve to remain calm soon failed, and we ended in full blown verbal combat.

Adolescence has been difficult for Roma. We all suffer when he fights for control. He can be defiant, argumentative, and manipulative when he demands to have his way. When he is less determined to be the boss, he reverts to the little boy I remember who is delightfully witty and charming, with a sweet spirit and a generous heart.

Bruce and I adopted Roma from Russia when he was seven and three-quarters—old enough for a strong personality to set. Until

God plucked him from the orphanage for our family, he was pretty much in control of his young life. It has been hard for him to hand the reins to us.

When I felt God's not-so-subtle call to adopt an older Russian child, I expected a shy, hurt little boy in need of gentle encouragement and acceptance. What God sent us was an assertive, confident little dictator! And God had a bigger surprise for me: I could love an adopted child every bit as much as I love my other three children. Little Roma was so cute and smiley, our older soft-hearted children often let him have his way. I was determined not to spoil him, especially when our son Taylor, twelve at the time of Roma's adoption, said that until he could think of him as a brother, he was going to consider Roma an "exchange student from God." Rearing a boy sent from God was a responsibility not to be taken lightly.

A determined mom and a headstrong boy often butt heads. This, like most of our battles, was a power struggle over who gets to be the boss. Once in my room, I fell to my knees and prayed through clinched teeth, "Lord, you sent him to us; pleeease help me deal with him. Please teach me patience and wisdom to mother Roma. And Lord, please give me *hope* that, in the long run, he will be okay."

I phoned a close friend that evening who I knew could provide hope. Her sons, age twenty-six and twenty-seven had challenged her similarly in their younger years, but were beginning to show signs of genuine maturity.

"This is so hard," I confessed. "I am praying that I keep my sanity, what little is left! But I am mostly praying that Roma will grow up to be a functioning member of society."

My compassionate and wise friend assured me that Roma would not always be fifteen. I ached at the thought that we might suffer another ten years before relief, but hope was hope, and I knew God's timing wasn't my timing; otherwise, Roma would be acting like an adult by now!

The next morning, I remembered a dream from the night before … Was it a dream? Bruce and I were talking to Roma outside in intense sunlight. Roma was like a dazzling white statue, yet he was moving and talking like normal. I had to squint to look at him. His essence was bathed in a white, unearthly brilliance. Bruce and I were talking about the bright light but were somehow not amazed by it. The dream was so vivid; it lingered with me throughout the day. I even asked Bruce, during a break from his and Roma's marathon snow shoveling, if we had indeed talked to Roma outside the day before, and had he been so bright we could hardly look at him? It almost seemed plausible because a record snowfall had begun days earlier. In the surreal time that we were trapped at home after the blizzard that week, our suburban neighborhood had been transformed into a winter wonderland. Everything was buried under four feet of snow after "once-in-a-hundred-years," back-to-back blizzards. When the sun reappeared, the whiteness of all that snow was truly blinding. Sunglasses were as essential as snow shovels. Despite the outside brilliance, Bruce's blank expression told me that no such thing as a conversation with a glowing white Roma had taken place.

That evening, having forgotten about my dream, I was catching up on my Bible reading. I began where I had left off, at Matthew, chapter seventeen, the Transfiguration. "His face shone like the sun, and his clothes became as white as the light … and a voice from the cloud said, 'This is my Son, whom I love; with him I am well pleased.'" (NIV)

Hairs stood up on my neck and chills raced down my arms.

Now don't get me wrong—I don't think for a moment that Roma is Jesus returning! But in the same way that we are all God's children, Roma is one of God's boys.

I had prayed for hope. Empowered with divine encouragement, I have lightened up with Roma and try to cut him some slack when he behaves like the adolescent that he is. It is his job as a teenager to test me at every turn, and he takes his business very seriously! Many of his strong-willed leadership "skills" will be assets to him when he grows into them. We need to be on the same team instead of on opposite sides at tug of war.

God is in control of Roma. Jesus was about thirty when he came into his ministry, not fifteen! The only knowledge we have of Jesus as a youth was that he was a determined lad, who didn't ask his parents' permission when he stayed behind in Jerusalem when they returned to Nazareth. Mary and Joseph reacted much better than I would have! Jesus was taking care of business, taking charge of his life. Like Roma does.

Roma is not stingy with his apologies. After another clash fueled by cabin fever, he came to me, humbly, like a little boy and confessed, "I just want to say I'm sorry." His repentant "I'm sorry" always mystifies me, from a confident boy who knows everything about everything. I am encouraged by the character it represents.

"Roma, I wish I could open the top of your head and pour in some of this wisdom I have gained in the years that it has taken me to become a dinosaur. Dad and I expect a lot of you because you are so gifted in so many areas. Before we are ready to let you go, you will be leaving us. We want you to be equipped to make it on your own. Kids leave home and forget the lessons their families try to teach. Many even walk away from their faith in God," I warned.

Roma's eyes narrowed as they met mine. "I could *never* not believe in God, after what He did for me," he said with that faint Russia accent that most people no longer detect.

I stared at my beautiful, angelic son, stunned. Roma was thankful after all. On some level, he *got it*.

God has renewed my hope. Even when slammed doors separate us, I still consider Roma one of my favorite surprise blessings.

I am clinging daily to God's promise, that He who began a good work will see it though, in Roma, and in me.

Thank you, Lord, for giving me hope. And Roma.

**Roman Sudzhashvili Michael, age 17, Fork
Union Military Academy, 2011**

Thanks...

Thanks to my family for having amazingly generous hearts. Your belief in this mission, starting with the adoption and continuing to the completion of this book, made the sharing of this story possible, and a joy.

The community of Mount Airy and Calvary United Methodist Church has been instrumental in supporting our family during the past ten years. It does indeed take a village to raise a child. Roma has felt the love of his extended family in this close-knit community.

Tremendous thanks especially go to my editor, Linda Morton. As small-world stories go, this is one I enjoy telling. Linda's family moved to Maryland in early 2002, a few months before we left for Russia, and will be moving back to North Carolina as this book goes to the publisher.

I introduced myself to a visitor at my church one Sunday morning. My new friend, Linda, revealed that she also was from North Carolina, and grew up twenty miles from my hometown of Burlington. As our conversation concentrated on our commonalities, I learned that she was married to a high-school friend of mine, and she had been a student at N.C. State while I was attending, living in the dorm next to mine. Twenty-some years later, we end up in a small Maryland town 300 miles from our hometowns, living a few miles apart. I didn't know at the time how helpful Linda would be in my life: Linda just happened to be an editor, and we were preparing to leave for Russia to adopt, as my story was unfolding.

Linda is first a friend, but she is also an awesome editor. She aggressively pulled more information out of me than I was aware was tucked inside, challenging me to connect seemingly unrelated parts. She encouraged me over the many years that the manuscript has lain dormant, except for occasional reading, sharing, updating, and Linda's re-editing. Linda's son, Lee, was the new boy in town until Roma arrived, and the two newcomers became the best of friends, and remain so. I am thankful that God put the Morton family in our community, our church, and our lives for the past ten years.

Bruce and Debbie, 2011

Made in the USA
Coppell, TX
20 October 2021

64389713R00135